Bolen
Advertising

3 0301 00023035 5

1984

ISTRUCTOR'S MANUAL

to accompany

ADVERTISING

WILLIAM H. BOLEN
Georgia Southern College

JOHN WILEY & SONS   NEW YORK
CHICHESTER BRISBANE TORONTO

LIBRARY
College of St. Francis
JOLIET, ILL.

Copyright © 1981 by John Wiley & Sons, Inc.

This material may be reproduced for testing or
instructional purposes by people using the text.

ISBN 0 471 08937 0

Printed in the United States of America

10 9 8 7 6 5 4 3 2 1

659.1
B687i

Preface

The function of an Instructor's Manual is to give you ideas and facts that will help you to better serve your students. Examination questions, comments for the end-of-chapter questions, and suggested solutions for the cases/experiential learning exercises are provided for your use. General ideas on how to improve your advertising course are also given for your consideration.

Thank you for taking the time to carefully examine <u>Advertising</u>. I welcome your comments, ideas, and suggestions on either the book or the instructor's manual. Your input will be most appreciated.

Advertising is an exciting subject and a fun course to teach. I hope you will let <u>Advertising</u> by Bolen be the vehicle you use to present the subject of advertising to your students.

Department of Marketing
Georgia Southern College
Statesboro, Georgia 30460
912-681-5336

William H. Bolen

Table of Contents

SECTION I

GENERAL RECOMMENDATIONS

To aid you in presenting the topic of advertising to your students, recommendations are given which pertain to the following areas:

COURSE OUTLINE

SUPPLEMENTARY READING MATERIALS

SPEAKERS - VISUAL AIDS - TRIPS

ADVERTISING PROJECT

OTHER SUGGESTIONS

COURSE OUTLINE

The following plans of organizations are for the most common time intervals in use at colleges and universities. The plans as given assume somewhat equal emphasis for all subject areas. They also assume that you will move straight through the text. Some instructors will, of course, want to place the topics in a different sequence. If such is the case, the appropriate outline can be adjusted to fit the particular need. In fact, the book is designed to allow for changes in sequence since there is much disagreement as to whether Message, Media, and Management should appear in that particular order or in some other order of presentation. It is recommended that the instructor try the order of sequence as presented in the text to see how well it works. In any event, the conceptual framework model as used in the text will allow for the message-media-management sequence to be changed without having an adverse effect on the model or the presentation of the material to the student.

Forty-eight class meetings
Three class meetings per week
Sixteen Week Semester

Week	Chapters To Be Covered
1	1-2
2	2-3
3	3
4	4-5
5	5-6
6	6-7
7	7-8
8	9-10
9	10-11
10	12-13
11	13-14
12	15-16
13	16-17
14	17-18
15	18-19
16	19-20

Fifty class meetings
Five class meetings per week
Ten Week Quarter

Week	Chapters To Be Covered
1	1-2
2	3-4
3	4-5
4	6-7
5	8-10
6	10-13
7	13-15
8	16-17
9	17-18
10	19-20

Thirty class meetings
Five class meetings per week
Six Week Session

Week	Chapters To Be Covered
1	1-3
2	4-6
3	6-10
4	10-13
5	14-16
6	17-20

Twenty-three class meetings
Three class meetings per week
Seven and One-Half Week Session

Week	Chapters To Be Covered
1	1-3
2	3-5
3	5-7
4	8-10
5	11-12
6	13-15
7	16-18
½	19-20

Forty-Two Class Meetings
Three class meetings per week
Fourteen Week Semester

Week	Chapters To Be Covered
1	1-2
2	2-3
3	3-4
4	5
5	6-7
6	7-8
7	9-10
8	10-11
9	12-13
10	13-14
11	15-16
12	16-17
13	17-18
14	19-20

SUPPLEMENTARY READING MATERIAL

Throughout the book, the reader is made aware of various advertising periodicals. In addition, the more common advertising periodicals are listed in the book's appendix. If funds are limited, it is strongly recommended that the one periodical that MUST be made available to students interested in advertising is Advertising Age. Through its special issues and supplements, it can bring the world of advertising to the classroom no matter where that classroom may be located. Some of the topics examined in detail in Advertising Age in the last twelve months are:

Sports Marketing	Test Marketing
Youth Marketing	Direct Marketing
Minority Marketing	Agrimarketing
Fashion Marketing	Health Care Marketing

Another possibility for supplemental reading is a book of readings on the subject of advertising. A check of book catalogs will reveal the names of several that are available. Most include the so-called classics as well as more current articles.

A third and, perhaps, more interesting idea from the students' viewpoint is to have students read some of the books which have been written by and/or about people who have been involved in the development of the advertising industry. Some of these books are:

Edward Buxton
Promise Them Anything
New York: Stein and Day
1972

Draper Daniels
Giants, Pigmies, and Other Advertising
  People
Illinois: Crain Communications, Inc.
1974

Fairfax M. Cone
The Blue Streak
Illinois: Crain Communications, Inc.
1973

Fairfax M. Cone
With All Its Faults
Massachusetts: Little, Brown and
    Company
1969

Jim Ellis
The Jumping Frog From Jasper County
New York: Abeland-Schuman Limited
1970

David Ogilvy
Confessions Of An Advertising Man
New York: Atheneum Press
1966

Maxwell Sackheim
My First Sixty Years In Advertising
New Jersey: Prentice-Hall, Inc.
1970

SPEAKERS - VISUAL AIDS - TRIPS

It is recommended that you make every effort to bring the real world into the classroom and vice-versa. Both you and your students will gain from this experience.

Speakers - There should be little difficulty in getting a speaker for an advertising class. Most media are happy to speak to advertising classes. In fact, some media trade groups, such as the Specialty Advertising Association International, have speakers' bureaus that will send people from the industry at no expense to talk to a class. In addition, local print and broadcast media will usually provide a speaker upon request to talk about the pros and cons of media. One possible idea is to set up a panel of speakers that represent various media and have them discuss the media they represent in the presence of the other media. Depending on the nature of the individuals involved, such a panel can be a very interesting experience for your students.

In addition to the media, two other sources of speakers are advertising agencies and advertising departments. In either case, the speaker should be encouraged to bring examples of his/her advertising work. Most speakers of this nature are free. Of greater importance is scheduling which if done well in advance may insure that the speaker will appear on campus. For schools not located in metropolitan areas it is hard to get an advertising person to come to campus. One way to overcome this hardship may involve finding out which agencies are used by firms in the area and then scheduling a visit by a speaker in conjunction with a planned call on the client. The same will be true for visits by advertising department personnel who make periodic visits to plant sites and similar company locations.

Still other possibilities for speakers are representives from various federal and state agencies as well as consumer groups. For example, a representative from the Federal Trade Commission can make the discussion of the material in Chapter 3 very interesting for the student.

Care should be taken not to have too many speakers. They should not be viewed as substitute teachers. Speakers should, instead, supplement the course material. Outside speakers can bring both knowledge and variety into the classroom. Anything done in excess can be a problem. For some advertising instructors, too many speakers has resulted in an advertising course that does not cover in sufficient detail the various aspects of advertising.

<u>Visual Aids</u> - Films, filmstrips, and slides may all be used to present the topic of advertising. In some cases, video cassettes are also a possibility. Due to the nature of the subject, numerous films are available for a substantial fee. Some, however, are free or can be used for a minimum fee:

>   <u>Volkswagen Advertising Campaign</u> - depicts the history of Volkswagen advertising. No longer available from Volkswagen but probably available on loan from a school in your area.

>   <u>Smirnoff Campaign</u> - A 1979 release that explains how a campaign is put together. Only expense is return postage. Available through Target Distribution, 509 Madison Avenue, New York, NY 10022.

>   <u>Dateline: Today</u> - Explains the operation of the Audit Bureau of Circulations. Available free to college members of ABC. College membership is $5 per year.

For films on the <u>Jack Daniels</u> advertising campaign and other marketing topics, contact: (only expense is return postage)

>   Modern Talking Picture Service, Inc.
>   2323 New Hyde Park Road
>   New Hyde Park, NY 11040

In addition to films and other standard visuals, the advertising instructor should always be in the process of collecting visual aids to use in the classroom. For example, a mat and a slick are both illustrated in the book but nothing beats showing your students the actual thing. With only limited effort, an advertising instructor can bring the student closer to the real world with the use of visuals in the classroom.

<u>Trips</u> - Where possible, at least once during the term, the classroom should move to the real world. A trip to an automated radio station or to a newspaper advertising department can show the media in action. In addition, a visit to an advertising agency or department can help the student get a better understanding of the advertising process. In any event, the students should be briefed before the trip on topics to be covered so that they will know what to expect. As a follow-up, a written report on the trip by each student is a suggested approach for getting good student involvement.

Another possibility for a trip may be a visit to a meeting of the local Advertising Club if one is located in your area. Some advertising clubs also offer a Career Day which might include visits to agencies/departments/media along with a program on careers in advertising. Ask various people in advertising in your area about the existence of an ad club. It could offer many benefits for your students.

ADVERTISING PROJECT

The best way to learn advertising is to do it. The advertising project can be as simple or as complex as the instructor wishes to make it. It can involve the development of a national campaign for a project or be local in nature. It can also involve having the student make up a product, name it, and develop ads for it for use in ten different media. As detailed in Case 10 in the book, for large projects you can divide your class into "agencies" and have them compete with each other for the best campaign. Or, as is the case with the ten ads, each student can work individually on the project.

The project can also be conducted as a public service project for the college or university. An ad campaign that sells your town as a place to shop to surrounding towns can be developed and then presented to appropriate groups such as the Chamber of Commerce or merchants association. Another idea is to sell the college itself. As a project, have your students develop an advertising campaign to attract students to the college or even a particular type of student. In most cases, it is assumed that the media will be paid as opposed to public service advertising.

Yet another idea, if college or university policy permits, is to do a real campaign for a real client. Some institutions have restrictions on projects that compete with private enterprise. Others have no such policy unless a fee is charged the client. If there are no institutional restrictions and the Department that houses the advertising course has a "foundation" account or some other account for unrestricted funds, the instructor can bring real-life problems into the classroom while generating funds for use by the department by having the advertising client "donate" funds to the department for services rendered.

If time is limited or the course is followed by an advertising campaign course which usually involves the development of a campaign, the project in the introductory advertising course may be less complex than those outlined above. The project might involve having each student bring to class current ads that illustrate various points as discussed in the text. This has proven to be a very effective assignment for building an illustration file for the instructor. On the negative side, library periodicals are where some students get their illustrations. Since the ads are cut out and brought to class, library materials can be damaged if students do not handle the assignment in an adult manner.

Another project involves a term paper on some aspect of advertising. Topics can range from the always popular "The Current State of Subliminal Advertising" to the "Use of Fear in Advertising." Papers that compare two media can also be interesting. If location permits, another good topic is to have the student choose an advertising agency and/or advertising department and study how it operates, what it does, etc. Note that these examples for term paper topics are not the traditional ones that can be researched in one afternoon in Readers Guide. Thought topics are considered more desirable from a learning standpoint.

Another idea is to have the student develop an annotated bibliography on a topic in advertising. The success of this project is somewhat a function of the library holdings that are available to the student. Depending on the wishes of the instructor, the student may create a type of term paper using the various references or the student may type up the various references on index cards for submission to the instructor. This assignment is very good when topics of current interest are selected. In some cases, the student may be asked to give a short oral presentation to the class on the topic covered by the annotated bibliography. For a different situation, each student may be asked to prepare a copy of his/her bibliography for distribution to each member of the class. This will create a source file for each student on current topics in advertising.

The various ideas as presented are not meant to be the only things that can be done as an advertising project. Your imagination is your only limit. You are, however, encouraged to make use of some type of project in your class since it will serve as a stimulus to the learning of the material in the textbook. In my own advertising classes, student evaluations time after time support the worth of the advertising project in some form.

OTHER SUGGESTIONS

By following the ideas already presented, you can be a more effective classroom teacher. You might also want to give some thought to pursuing some additional considerations that may be of assistance to you as an instructor in advertising.

For a fee of $25.00, payable to the American Association of Advertising Agencies (AAAA), 200 Park Avenue, New York, NY 10017, you can subscribe to their Education Service which sends to you the AAAA Headquarters Newsletter, Media Newsletter, Washington Newsletter, Advertising Campaign Report Newsletter and numerous bulletins on issues pertaining to advertising. It is noted that each month, the Advertising Campaign Report Newsletter presents a case history of a successful advertising program. Recent issues have featured campaigns for L'eggs Sheer Energy, American Greetings Corporation's Holly Hobbie, and the American Egg Board's "The Incredible Edible Egg." Each campaign report looks at areas such as background data, marketing considerations, marketing strategy, creative strategy, media strategy, and campaign results. Examples of actual ads are also included. Creative materials for classroom use are available for each campaign on a use and return basis from AAAA for a $5 deposit. The Advertising Campaign Report Newsletter is made available solely for institutional purposes. As such, it can be reproduced for classroom distribution without permission of AAAA.

For an annual fee of $5.00, payable to the Audit Bureau of Circulations, 900 North Meacham Road, Schaumburg, Illinois 60195, your institution can become an Academic Associate member of ABC. As such, you will be able to obtain numerous examples of ABC Reports for classroom use as well as the use of a film on how ABC works entitled DATELINE: TODAY as was noted earlier. Your membership also entitles you to attend the ABC annual meetings and to receive various ABC publications.

For an annual fee of $50.00, payable to the Direct Mail/Marketing Association, 6 East 43rd Street, New York, New York 10017, your institution can become an educational member of DMMA. As such you will receive the revised Direct Mail/Marketing Manual which contains a great wealth of information about direct marketing. Also included in the fee are a subscription to Direct Marketing, and the Association's monthly newsletter, Direct Marketing Journal. The advertising instructor is also encouraged to apply for a fellowship to attend a DMMA sponsored Basic Direct Marketing Institute which is presented several times each year. The all-expense-paid trip is a very informative 3½ day meeting. Two or three instructors usually get invited to these seimnars which are also attended by direct mail practitioners. This should not be confused with a different seminar offered by DMMA for students. Write DMMA at the above address for more information.

The Specialty Advertising Association International, 1404 Walnut Hill Lane, Irving, Texas 75062, offers a program twice a year at its trade shows, entitled VIP (Very Important Professor) Seminar, where about 12 to 15 instructors are invited to hear a discussion on specialty advertising and to visit the floor of the trade show. The all-expense-paid program is very informative and results in very unique specialty samples being given to the instructor for later use in the classroom. Further information can be obtained from SAAI. It is noted that Specialty Advertising Report, a quarterly publication of SAAI is sent to all instructors who have attended a VIP Seminar. Others may request that they be placed on the mailing list for this publication.

Trade Associations are additional sources of information for the instructor of advertising. It is recommended that you write to each of the associations listed in the Appendix requesting that they send to you appropriate information on advertising. Explain to them that you teach advertising. You should get much information since it is to their advantage to have their areas presented in a favorable way in your class.

As an instructor of advertising it is recommended that you become an active member of the American Academy of Advertising. In addition to the normal benefits that come with this type of membership (Journal of Advertising, annual meeting, etc.), the Academy, in conjunction with AAAA, offers a five-day training program for new advertising educators. Special fellowships to Ad Age's Advertising Week are also made available through the Academy. For more information, contact the Journal of Advertising, 395 JKB, Brigham Young University, Provo, Utah 84602. This publication can provide you with the name and address of the current Treasurer of the Academy who can be contacted for more information. Annual dues (1980) are $25.

Along with the above efforts that make you more informed about national advertising, learning will also be enhanced if you make a practice of relating current ads in use in your area to the lecture material. Make yourself aware of local advertising. As a general rule, students prefer instructors who do not always use a General Motors type example. Attempt to balance your presentation with a good mix of the two. Your lectures will gain credibility when you integrate local examples in with the text materials.

No effort has been made to include all possible things you might do to make your advertising class the best class you ever taught. Each person who uses Advertising by Bolen is faced with different constraints. Due to these different teaching environments, some things that have been suggested will not work for you. But don't assume they will not work. Try them! Try your own ideas! Be innovative! Always be willing to change your approach if it will result in a stronger advertising class. As an advertising instructor, part of your time is spent telling your students to be creative. Practice what you preach.

Remember--good teaching is an on-going challenge.

SECTION II

SUGGESTED ANSWERS
TO
DISCUSSION QUESTIONS

The questions at the end of each chapter are designed to reenforce the material which is presented in the chapter. Some require the student to reexamine basic concepts while others require research and/or application of the material. These questions can be used as a homework assignment, take-home quiz, review exercise, or even as a regular exam.

CHAPTER 1 - ADVERTISING: AN OVERVIEW

1-1   Advertising is any controlled form of nonpersonal presentation and promotion of ideas, goods, or services by an identified sponsor that is used to inform and persuade a selected market. For purposes of explanation, the definition can be analyzed as follows:

Controlled - Most advertising is paid for, thereby giving control to the advertiser. Some advertising of a public service nature, even though not paid for, may still be controlled.

Nonpersonal - Advertising is not personal selling. It should be aimed at a target market but it cannot be expected to be tailored to each individual as is possible with personal selling. Much advertising can be considered mass communication.

Ideas, goods, and services - Advertising can sell something besides soap and other products. A service company such as a bank or laundry can use advertising as can any nonprofit organization that wishes to sell an idea. Even politicians use advertising to sell their ideas and services.

Identified sponsor - Advertising identifies the sponsor whereas propaganda does not. No advertiser wishes to advertise without identifying the source. It would be foolish to advertise a product, yet not tell people where to get it.

Inform - Advertising that is effective should aid in the search process by telling that something exists and how it can help them.

Persuade - Advertising should sell. Persuasion is the heart of advertising and one of its main problems. Without persuasion, procrastination would overrule any positive effect that informing customers might have on the market.

Selected market - Although nonpersonal in nature, effective advertising cannot appeal to everyone with a single advertisement. Carefully prepared ads placed in carefully selected media hopefully will reach the target market with the desired effect.

In regard to the last part of the question, for those definitions that are different, most will tend to emphasize the mass communication aspect of the topic. If this is the case, it can be said that mass communication is included in the definition in the text since such media are certainly nonpersonal in nature.

1-2   Publicity and advertising are related but are not synonymous. Publicity is defined as the development and placement of information before the public in a nonpromotional format (e.g., a news story). Advertising as defined in Question 1 above is, of course, promotional. Both are a part of the promotional mix and, therefore, should be coordinated. The two also differ in terms of control. Since most advertising is paid placement, the organization can say where such ads should be placed. As for publicity, although written by the advertiser, its placement decision normally rests with the media.

1-3   Few advertisements should appeal to everyone because few target markets are defined as a truly mass market. Advertisements should direct their efforts toward the target market. The primary customer for a new car, store, restaurant, or any other product, service, or idea is a person for whom the advertisement is developed and the media selected. Others may also buy but the primary goal is the target market. In advertising, a good approach to follow is the rifle approach as opposed to the shotgun approach. The smart advertiser takes aim on the carefully selected market instead of advertising to just anyone.

1-4   Advertising is not a recent development. Although difficult to document, advertising symbols and signs probably date back to the earliest civilizations that had any type of primitive commerce. It is known that signs, trademarks, and town criers date back hundreds of years. Evidence of signs has been found in the ruins of Pompeii. One sign found in a sidewalk even advertised a house of ill repute (not mentioned in book). As for trademarks, the Middle Ages saw these marks come into use to identify each Guild. Also, it is known that at least by 1141, town criers were in use in France. Other dates of significance in the early history of advertising are:

    1450   Gutenberg Bible - movable type
    1480   Caxton handbill - first advertisement
    1591   First newspaper ad

1-5   This question can be done individually or as a class or team assignment. As a class, you might wish to assign each student to contact appropriate sources in the area and find out the history behind the media. The results can then be combined so that a history of advertising for the area is compiled. Not only can the results be quite interesting, but it could result in a publication for you if you choose to write up the findings for a local interest publication. As for comparing the findings to the history of advertising in the United States, a side-by-side comparison is suggested. For example, the first radio station (1920 - KDKA) can be compared to when the first station in your area came on the air. In conjunction with radio, it might be interesting to also find out when that first local station joined a network and how the network-local mix has changed over time. In every instance, dates and development should be compared. The complexity and depth of answer to this question will naturally be a function of where you are and how broad an area you wish to cover with your class.

1-6   As with question 5, this can be done individually or as a class or team assignment. If most media are not in your area and your library holdings are limited, this question should not be attempted if you are teaching the course in a short session. If time permits, the above problems can be overcome by contacting various trade groups for information. Sufficient lead time will be needed, however, to give the trade associations time to respond (see Appendix C for selected sources).

1-7   Does advertising create demand? Does it stimulate demand? Does it make people buy something they do not need or want? Questions such as these can be answered with either a yes or a no depending on how one wishes to interpret the various findings that are available. Many people argue that advertising cannot create demand but it can stimulate it. Every advertiser should attempt to persuade people to act, thereby stimulating demand. But the number of product failures would tend to make a person conclude that stimulation will not work if no true demand is present. As a counter argument, it is said that advertising can create peer pressure, especially in the young and/or lower demographic market, thereby making people buy clothes, applicances, etc. that they have no need for or cannot afford. For a given person, such a situation is possible. It is very difficult to prove one way or the other whether the advertisement created a demand for a product or simply stimulated a latent desire for it.

1-8   Advertising is an expense which must be paid for. This true statement may or may not cause costs and prices to be higher. There are two schools of thought for this question. One approach states that prices will rise since advertising will not have sufficient impact on demand to compensate for its cost. The opposite approach takes the argument that stimulated demand results in higher production levels which results in the spreading of overhead which results in lower per unit costs. And, therefore, a lower price. In addition to this traditional two-sided discussion, studies at the "middleman" level reveal that the level of advertising at this point in the distribution channel also may have an impact on price. By having your students conduct a search of the literature, this question should result in much discussion but no clear-cut answer.

1-9   Phillip Nelson believes that advertising increases consumer information about substitutes thereby reducing monopoly power. If one disagrees with his statement, the person probably believes that advertising may help to create brand loyalty, stabilize the market, and reduce the chance for greater competition. As is true with the previous two questions, much discussion can result from this question, particularly if your students are directed to go and find various sources that will support the two schools of thought that prevail within the answer.

1-10 Trends shown in the data include:
(A)   A growing role in the media mix for television
(B)   A diminishing yet still dominant role for newspapers
(C)   An increase in actual dollars spent for all media (inflation is a factor)
(D)   A diminishing importance for farm media as more people live off the farm
(E)   A changing role for national advertising within the various media
The trends as cited as well as others may change significantly in the next several years. It is recommended that you update these tables for your class or have them go to Advertising Age and do it themselves. Cable T.V., electonic newspapers, and changing consumer habits and life styles along with other considerations should reflect themselves in these tables in the future. The impact of change is always interesting to observe.

CHAPTER 2 - ADVERTISING: ITS RELATIONSHIP TO MARKETING

2-1   As a philosophy of management, the marketing concept is defined as a state of mind in a company that results in all plans, policies, procedures, and actions of the company being customer-oriented. It should be noted that the marketing concept does not say that you should not make a profit. An obvious assumption of any marketing situation is continuity of the firm which requires a profit. If a firm, on the other hand, develops a philosophy of the "customer be damned," profits may exist in the short-term but cease in the longterm. Almost all marketing situations require repeat visits by customers to continue in business. The philosophy behind the marketing concept works to encourage this repeat patronage and continued profit. It is noted that some say that the marketing concept is no longer a viable concept. In most cases, the ideas that are presented use semantics to disapprove its validity. If viewed as a philosophy, the concept appears to be as valid today as it ever was and will be for years to come. If viewed in a human sense, any marketing decision may not agree with the wishes of a particular consumer. If such is the case, that consumer will agree that the firm in question, obviously, does not believe in the marketing concept. It is noted that a firm pursuing the marketing concept will develop ads which the customer will be attracted to that sell what the customer will have a need or desire to have. Such ads will then be placed in the media that the target market prefers. It is emphasized that the advertiser may not like the ads, the product, or the selected media. The decisions were made on the basis of customer preference, not advertiser preference.

2-2   The target market as described is too broad. Such a description of the market does not help the advertiser in any way to develop the advertising message or select the media. It is, of course, also unrealistic to believe that <u>everyone</u> is a market for <u>anything</u>. In the definition of advertising, advertising attempts to inform and persuade the selected market. The owner of the health food chain should study carefully the demographics and psychographics of the people who buy such products so that a profile of the health food customer can be created. This profile can then be used in the development of the advertising message as well as in media selection.

2-3   The business market can be divided in four categories: trade, industrial, professional, and institutional. Each of these business types has different needs which are reflected in the advertising which is developed to reach them.
    Trade: firms that sell to the ultimate consumer. Advertisements directed to this market stress how the item advertised can help the store sell to the ultimate consumer and/or how the item has been presold in some way to the consumer market.
    Industrial: firms that sell to the other business markets or to another member of the industrial market. The means of production as well as the produced items themselves may be marketed. Derived demand is a significant factor in this market. In some cases, consumer advertising is undertaken to encourage demand which hopefully will be reflected in the industrial market demand for a product.
    Professional: firms/individuals who endorse or recommend products. Advertisements combine with personal selling in an attempt to obtain an acceptance of the product by the medical doctor, professor, etc.
    Institutional: firms who sell a service as their primary product. Advertising appeals concentrate on how the advertised item can assist in providing the needed service, whether it be for a restaurant or a cleaning service. Although many of these same products may also be marketed to the consumer market by means of the trade market, institutional products will generally be sold in larger containers and move through different channels. The physical product is the same but the advertising approach will be different.

2-4   The statement makes little sense unless it is talking about the professional market. If a medical doctor can be "sold" on the idea of a particular drug by means of advertising, personal selling, and free samples, the end result may be many prescriptions being written for the drug which, naturally, result in many sales. The same is true for anyone who is in a position of leadership where others "must" follow. Corporate presidents and college professors receive many books free. Publishers do not mind this practice, however, because they know that an endorsement or adoption by either will result in numerous units of the product being sold.

2-5   Each class of consumer goods is marketed differently and, therefore, is advertised differently.
    Convenience goods: an item that is relatively inexpensive, is purchased on a recurring basis, and is dependent on place availability.
        Staple - major manufacturer advertising effort is required to establish a market for a particular brand of milk, bread, etc. Product is available at numerous competing outlets. Most advertisements stress brand awareness and repeat purchase.
        Impulse - no purchase was planned by the customer. Point-of-purchase advertising strategically placed is essential (A Coke purchased for consumption while shopping).

          Emergency - within reason, price or brand are not major factors. Place
              availability in relation to need is primary consideration. (A broken fan
              belt may be fixed as a result of an ad in the <u>Yellow Pages</u>.)
       Shopping goods: Goods which are studied by the customer before a purchase is
         made (clothing, furniture, etc.).
         Homogenous - price is only product differential.
         Heterogeneous - numerous differences which make comparisons difficult.
         Whenever possible, advertising generally aims at creating a heterogeneous
         shopping good out of a homogenous one. It then works to sell the particular
         benefits of the heterogeneous good so as to promote customer awareness of the
         particular brand.
       Specialty goods: Goods that have no substitutes in the eyes of the target market.
         Some advertisements encourage customers to "accept no substitutes." Although
         many specialty goods are regarded as luxury items, the true test is not price
         or image - it is substitutability.
       Unsought goods: Goods that are traditionally not sought after by the target market.
         Emotional appeals are normally used to support the necessary personal selling
         effort that is needed to sell such products as insurance and encyclopedias.

2-6   For a routine reorder of paper supplies, the purchasing agent may be the only
person to be sold. On the other hand, the sale of an installation, accessory
equipment, raw materials, component parts, and even types of supplies in many
industrial situations involves selling everyone from the company president on down
including the purchasing agent. To sell a machine may involve selling the machine
operator, the plant engineer, the production manager and others depending on the
situation. Advertisements placed in the media that these decisionmakers are
exposed to can help sell the product.

2-7   A marketing program results in a product being sold at a given price at a
particular place as a result of various promotional efforts. The end effect of
these elements is an image that over time can help or hinder the marketing
effort.
        Product - What is sold - good, service, and/or idea
        Price - Projected market value
        Place - Distribution - where is product available
        Promotion - Advertising, personal selling, sales promotion, publicity
        Personality - Image - how the product and/or company is perceived by the
          customer. Considered by some to be the result of the marketing mix,
          instead of a part of it.
All elements in the mix are equally important. If one element is weaker than
the rest, however, it might be thought to be the most important until the problem
can be corrected.

2-8   Each student will probably tailor his/her answer to go along with the sixteen
guidelines given in the textbook but with adjustments for what they already know
about the subject. You can use this question in its place in Chapter 2 and again
at the end of the course to see how the answers change over time. It is the stated
goal of <u>Advertising</u> by Bolen to meet the objective of understanding advertising as
presented in the conceptual framework for the book. With your help as an
instructor, we should see significant movement toward understanding as the student
moves through the course.

2-9   Depending on the firms selected, the answer to this question can be almost
anything. The exercise should, however, reenforce the idea that the consumer
market and business market are quite different. It is noted that the last part

of the question may result in some suggestions that are not realistic. Attempt to redirect the student's efforts toward something that can be done within the resource limits of the firm.

2-10 By its nature, the farm market is a business market and a consumer market. It is also very conservative. With a "prove it" or "show me" attitude, it is very difficult to sell to the farm market. Due to differences in geography, the media must also be carefully selected so as to use the ones that sell a local area. Advertising to this market is different, but even more so if the advertiser has limited experience in this market. Care should be taken never to "talk down" to the farm market. With a "typical" tractor costing $40,000, the farmer is not in a market that can be taken lightly.

CHAPTER 3 - EXTERNAL ADVERTISING RESTRAINTS

3-1 The question can result in a term paper assigmnent for the class if depth is desired. A brief answer would probably cite the following legislation along with several FTC decisions that have resulted in firms making significant changes in their advertising programs.

1914 Federal Trade Commission Act - created the Federal Trade Commission. Objective was to curb unfair competitive practices in the marketplace.

1938 Wheeler-Lea Amendment to the Federal Trade Commission Act - FTC could now act if an ad was thought to be unfair or deceptive in its own right.

1974 Federal Trade Commission Improvement Act - FTC could now draft rulings that affect commerce before the fact as opposed to having to wait until a firm committed an act that was thought to be deceptive or unfair.

It should be obvious to the student that the FTC has a significant impact on how the advertiser projects his product to the customer.

3-2 The Wheeler-Lea Amendment earned its name as the Truth In Advertising Act because it removed the requirement that limited "unfair" to mean harmful to a competing firm. With the passage of the Amendment, any advertisement that was deceptive or unfair because of what was stated or what was left unstated was ruled to be a violation of the law.

3-3 A list of Federal Trade Commission Actions can be developed from various sources. The Wall Street Journal and Advertising Age are two sources for very recent actions. Another source is Federal Trade Commission Decisions, a government publication. As a possible class assignment, you might alter the question and have each team of students or each student, depending on the class size, take a particular year and make note of all FTC actions that pertained to advertising. This exercise can be used to reenforce the information that was used to answer question 3-1.

3-4 As noted in the Statute, any advertisement that sells, disposes of, or promotes a product by means of print media while, at the same time, presenting an assertion, representation, or statement of fact which is untrue, deceptive, or misleading, is illegal. As discussed in the text, for the Statute to apply, the person, organization, etc. who develops the advertisement must do so with the intent to sell the product or to dispose of it. To overcome the problem of intent, as well as the implication that the Statute only applies to print media, the AAF Model Statute simply states, "False, misleading, or deceptive acts or practices in the conduct of any trade or commerce are hereby declared illegal." All loopholes in the Printers' Ink Statute were taken care of as well as much wordiness with the creation of the AAF Model Statute.

3-5 The purpose of the National Advertising Review Board is to take action as required on complaints about specific advertising practices. Many such complaints originate with competitors of the accused or by means of consumer complaints to a local Better Business Bureau. The complaints are then analyzed by the National Advertising Division (NAD) for validity as outlined in Figure 3-4 in the text. If no solution can be reached, the NARB itself will then act on the complaint by setting up a five-member panel (three advertisers, one agency person, and one public person) who will study the situation and make recommendations. It is noted that all actions of the NAD and NARB are public and that most advertisers cooperate with the procedure. In the first five years (1971-1976) that the NARB operated, only 18 cases out of 1174 complaints were not successfully handled within the framework of the Board - a significant accomplishment for a Board with no actual legal power.

3-6 Established in 1952, the T.V. Code is concerned with the broad spectrum of television problems. As for advertising, the code limits the number of minutes of advertising per hour for various categories of programming as well as the content of the ads themselves. As the Instructor's Manual is written, the controversy continues over how much advertising to permit per hour. A check of Advertising Age should reveal the current status of this decision as well as any actions that have been taken on requests by advertisers to alter the Code. As an additional assignment, you might ask selected students to go to television stations in the area as well as major advertisers and solicit their opinions about the Code. Also, if you have a television station in your area that operates as a non-code station, you might compare its programming and advertisements with code stations.

3-7 The Creative Code as published by the American Association of Advertising Agencies in 1962 recognizes in writing the potential impact of advertising on the American way of life and then pledges not to encourage the development of misleading ads or ads that might offend or ads that might not reflect all the true facts of a situation. The Code as stated provides a standard of performance for advertising agencies to follow as they develop advertisements for clients. Of course, any agency, advertiser, or anyone involved in advertising can make use of the Code as an ethical guideline. If carefully adhered to by all in advertising, the Creative Code would eliminate some of the problems that are found in advertising today.

3-8 If advertisers have an understanding of consumer behavior, then the overall effect of their advertising should be enhanced.
   Motive - A need or desire that causes a person to act. May be rational or emotional in nature. It is observed that once a need is met or satisfied, it loses its significance as a motivator.
   Learning - Changes in responses and response tendencies due to the effects of experience. Tools of learning include repetition and contiguity (associating a product with a desirable situation).
   Attitude - A learned tendency to respond in a given manner to a particular situation. May wish to change an attitude or take advantage of it.
   Perception - How one interprets a situation as a result of various stimuli. Does a particular customer see an ice cream cone as a treat or as something to make one gain weight?
The four elements as listed have a direct bearing on how an individual reacts in a situation, including one that involves advertising. As for examples, any advertisement can be analyzed in relation to the four factors. In fact, you might choose to make this question a class assignment and have each person select an ad for purposes of study and then write up how it illustrates the various points.

3-9   Reference groups are important to all advertisers. Those people with whom customers identify play a major role in determining what people want and/or buy. Each different customer group has its own unique reference groups that will serve to establish its norms of buyer behavior. Whether family-, club-, church-, or work-related, the reference group may unlock the door to a successful advertising program if proper analysis reveals its true makeup and beliefs.

3-10 The exercise as outlined will usually illustrate in a very clear way that people are different. If all the collected answers are combined, a more comprehensive study can be made of how occupation affects product choice or even, perhaps, how social class affects the purchase decision. Not only will one likely conclusion be that social classes do exist in your town, but also that they are different enough to be advertised to as separate entities.

CHAPTER 4 - THE ADVERTISING INDUSTRY

4-1   In an advertising department, the advertiser determines the advertising program and develops the advertisements whereas in an advertising agency, it is the agency that determines the advertising program in cooperation with the advertiser and develops the ads. The department and the agency may be considered the same if viewed as an in-house agency but they cannot in reality be the same since the true agency maintains a certain degree of independence as a result of its <u>agency</u> relationship.

4-2   An advertising department may be set up on the basis of customer group, geography, or product group, as well as by advertising function. Any of these approaches or some combination thereof, will provide the advertiser with an advertising department that should yield the desired level of specialization for the given set of circumstances.

4-3   The brand manager approach represents more than an advertising department. Under this concept, the brand manager is held accountable in the functional sense for both the advertising and marketing of the product. The brand manager must work closely with the marketing staff and other brand managers of the company so that effective coordination can be achieved. At the same time, brand managers within the company may be competing against each other along with outside competitors for selected markets. Unless everyone in the company has a complete understanding of functional authority, the end result of this highly competitive environment can be chaos.

4-4   A full-service agency is required under AAAA service standards to provide the following seven services:
1. Study the product - Learn its advantages and disadvantages along with that of the competition.
2. Study the present and potential market - Who is the actual as well as potential target market? What are seasonal and geographic factors that might affect the market?
3. Understand the factors of distribution - How can the product be moved profitably to the point of sale? The full-service agency will interview all elements within the channel in an effort to learn more about the product.
4. Understand the media - Media availability, reach, and cost are three of numerous factors that need to be understood prior to media selection.
5. Formulation of advertising plan - Plan includes, in part, the appeals to be used, advertising messages to be employed, media to be used, and any

merchandising factors to be employed.

6. Execution of the plan - With the advertising plan having been approved by the client, advertisements must now be prepared, space and time must be bought and verified, and finally, the client must be billed.

7. Cooperate with other marketing units - Since advertising is part of marketing, the full-service agency may have ideas that can assist one or more departments within the company (may or may not be related to advertising). It will offer such advice to such departments as well as coordinate its activities with them.

4-5 Why use a full-service agency? Ten reasons as provided by AAAA are:

1. Centralization of authority and responsibility - One entity is to blame or is due proper credit depending on the success or failure of an advertisement.

2. Simplified coordination and administration - It is easy for an advertiser to work with just one agency that handles all of the advertising tasks.

3. Greater objectivity - A well-studied market and product should allow the agency to do a better job of developing a sound advertising program.

4. Sales-oriented creative work - The full-service agency never loses sight of the fact that the purpose of advertising is to sell the product.

5. Synergistic experience - The experience gained from working with other clients and products may result in a better campaign.

6. Stronger pool of talent - By having all advertising functions under one roof, the resulting available expertise allows the full-service agency to react quickly to any situation or problem.

7. Professional strength in marketing area - people who have worked or are working in full-service agencies learn marketing by doing. This expertise flows to other companies as people move about in their professional careers.

8. May be less expensive - By having the campaign done under one roof, it will normally be better than a piecemeal effort. Economies of scale may also result in more advertising effort per dollar by using a full-service agency.

9. Simplifies corrective changes - If the campaign is piecemeal, then corrections will also be piecemeal. If a full-service agency is used, all corrections, changes, and so forth, can be made under one roof.

10. Better working environment - The "creative" atmosphere of a full-service agency may attract better people as well as make them more productive. The end product of this situation is, hopefully, a better advertising campaign.

4-6 Compensation for advertising agencies comes from three sources: commissions, charges, and fees. As for commissions, agencies will normally receive 15 percent commission for national advertising which is placed in most mass media (16 2/3% for outdoor). Charges for services (photography, artwork, etc.) usually range in the area of cost plus 15 percent to 20 percent. Fees may also be charged for certain noncommission media (for example, direct mail) or for nonadvertising services (such as marketing research or public relations). The alternative to this system is a complete fee system which removes commissions as a decision factor. As noted in question 4-7, the fee system removes the temptation to select those media that give the more favorable commission rates.

4-7 Under the fee system, the agency quotes a total fee for services rendered. All commissions, fees, and charges will be absorbed by this one fee. Any excess commissions (technically all commissions) will be rebated to the advertiser. It is believed that the fee system promotes professionalism in advertising since it relieves the temptation to select media on the basis of the commission rate. The commission system, on the other hand, is a well understood, time-tested system. Although it is predicted that the fee system will replace the commission system at some time in the future, most major advertisers have made no move in that direction since the commission system allows them to fund their advertising within the constraints of the current method of compensation. The smaller firms, on the other hand, are having to go with the fee system in order to get an agency to handle the account. Commissions alone will not allow the appropriate funding level for most small advertising accounts. Is fee or commission a better system? For those advertisers with an option, the fee system through its professional approach to advertising probably has the edge over the commission-charges-fees approach.

4-8   Special service groups provide expertise for the advertiser, agency, or media, whenever a "special" task is called for. The most common special service groups are in the area of printing - typographers, photoengravers, and printers. Other examples are firms that create radio and/or television commercials, photographers, modeling agencies, and advertising researchers.

4-9   Depending on the situation, the answer may be Yes or No. The advertiser must remember that the media salesperson is a commission salesperson first and a creator of advertising second. Also, the media salesperson and those who work for the media may know little or nothing about advertising. Under these conditions, should an advertiser put his/her advertising in the hands of the media? Note that some media do a good job. Also, some advertisers know little about advertising themselves. The choices may be limited for the firm that is too small for an agency. But being small should not be equated with having a poor advertising effort. When using the media as a creator of advertising, the advertiser should work with the media and insist that the media make every effort to make each advertisement the best possible. It is noted that the advertiser should also not expect the media to recommend not using itself in the advertiser's media mix. It is this lack of objectivity coupled with the lack of advertising expertise that makes relying on the media to develop advertising a situation that is full of problems. If no alternatives are possible, the advertiser should proceed into the situation with caution.

4-10   If the class is large and the number of resources are few, you might assign only one firm to a student or a student team and then have a discussion in class that will bring out what the various organizations had to say about the advertising industry. An alternative to this question is to invite to the classroom, a representative from each of the four groups to sit down with the class and discuss the advertising industry as it exists in your area. Such a discussion can be quite informative if the industry participants are knowledgeable about their part of the industry but are not too protective of their one end of the business.

CHAPTER 5 - ADVERTISING FOUNDATION

5-1   Communication is defined as the mutual interchange of ideas by any effective means. For an advertiser to communicate, ideas must be sent (advertisement) by an effective means (media) so that the customer can react as reflected in market behavior (buy the product). If any part of the communication process fails, then the advertising effort fails. Good advertisements in the right media that are aimed at the wrong customers spell failure. Good advertisements designed for the right customers that are placed in the wrong media are also a problem. Finally, the correct media for the right target market will not compensate for poor advertisements. Good advertising is good communication. By understanding the communication process, the advertiser is made cognizant of the fact that good advertising means working with the various communication elements to insure that each part of the communication process is viable. Good communication is only as strong as the weakest element in the communication process.

5-2   Market analysis encompasses learning about the total market for the item to be advertised, the role that competition plays in that market, and the market's characteristics. As for product analysis, it evaluates the product's identifying symbols, package, and physical characteristics. The advertiser can and should utilize both product analysis and market analysis. By following this course of action, a proper foundation will be available upon which to build an advertising program.

5-3   The data sources will be a function of the product that is selected. Possible sources include trade publications, trade associations, media, bureaus of government, and information that is for sale to the advertiser. Such data may be used to learn as much as possible about the market for the product. By knowing the market, the advertiser can better select the advertising appeals to be used, the media to carry the message, and all other aspects of the campaign. Before many decisions can be made, the advertiser must have a well-thought-out definition of the market.

5-4   A trademark is any word, name, symbol, or device, or any combination thereof adopted for and used by a manufacturer or merchant to identify his goods and distinguish them from those manufactured by others. A service mark, on the other hand, is any mark used in the sale or advertising of services to identify such services and to distinguish them from the services of others by means such as marks, names, symbols, designations, slogans, titles, and distinctive features of radio or other advertising used in commerce. The essential difference between the two is that a trademark is for a product while a service mark is for a service. Also, trademarks must be affixed to the product while it is difficult to do the same with a service. Third, trademarks are registered with the Patent Office while service marks are filed with the Library of Congress. The best way to distinguish between the two is with an example. If the new Boeing 757 rolls off the assembly line with the Boeing name and symbol on the tail, this is a trademark. If the next plane coming off the line has the symbol and name of American Airlines, that plane carries a service mark since an airline sells a service, not planes.

5-5   "Smell" as a name for a deodorant literally "stinks!" The name has a negative connotation. It might also be considered to be descriptive. With such a name, the product will also lack prestige. In fact, the only thing that could be said that is positive is that the name would be distinctive. Of course, distinctiveness may not lead to sales in this situation. Obviously, another name needs to be developed for the product. What should that name be? Near You, Together, and Just You are three possible names. Why not let your students creativity come up with various names for the deodorant.

5-6   A trade character can be used for continuity purposes in a campaign. They can also help sell a product, generate interest for the particular program, or serve numerous other functions. Of course, the trade character should serve to support the product - never detract from it. If possible, a trade character should not be a contemporary person since contemporary trade characters must be updated from time to time to maintain their contemporary nature. Should a firm use a trade character? There is no clear-cut answer. Firms are now beginning to use more of them. Recent additions to the active trade character list are RCA and Borden.

5-7 Protection and Promotion are the two basic functions of a package. Both are essential to the successful marketing of a product. A torn package hurts the value of the product. A stale product is not a successful product. Cost of protective packaging can be high but can be well worth it. As for promotion, it should be remembered that the product and the package are usually synonymous in the minds of customers. A package may be designed to sell to two different markets, may give the product added marketability, should not make the product obsolete before its time, and may offer a combination offer of two related products. Good packaging can help sell a product. Poor packaging can destroy a product before it has a chance to be a success.

5-8 The comment is referring to a pull strategy of advertising where the manufacturer advertises his product directly to the market as compared to a push strategy where the advertiser places his message before the channel who in turn advertises the product to the market. If a manufacturer wants to insure that his product will be positioned properly, the necessary dollars for pull advertising must be made available. Under a push strategy, positioning in the consumer market will be more or less left up to the "middlemen" with guidance coming from the manufacturer. Procter & Gamble is the classic example for pull advertising. As for push, most manufacturers follow this approach out of necessity since the dollars required for a pull strategy are too great for most firms' financial resources.

5-9 As discussed in the text, there are eleven advertising objectives given that might be used by an advertiser. These are:
   Induce Trial – get people to try the advertised item.
   Intensify Usage – get users of a product to buy more of a product. There is no better prospect for a product than a current user.
   Sustain Preference – remind users of the product on a regular basis.
   Confirm Imagery – advertising can help to promote as well as reenforce an image.
   Change Habits – advertising may be used to help sell an idea that is not common to the market such as the one card habit as sold by Visa and MasterCard.
   Build Line Acceptance – companies may work to sell their total line. Hunt's, K-Mart, and Kraft are just three examples of advertising campaigns that work to sell the product line while at the same time trying to sell individual products within the line.
   Break The Ice – some ads may be used to lay a foundation for a future marketing effort – Avon along with most insurance companies pursue this objective.
   Build Ambience – advertisements can be used to help build a positive feeling about a business.
   Generate Sales Leads – a prospect list can be the result of an advertising effort if ads work to solicit a response from the target market.
   Increase Awareness – all ads hopefully create awareness but some ads have awareness as their primary objective. Many public service advertisements may be found in this category.
   Increase Sales – a very common objective but not a good objective unless it can be made specific and, hopefully, quantified in some manner.
The question makes the request that five of the objectives should be listed and fully explained. The ads that are cited by your students as being examples of these objectives will probably also illustrate one or more additional objectives from among those that are listed. You might wish to select a cross-section of the

advertisements that are cited by your students and study them as a class in terms of what objectives are being served by each advertisement.

5-10 Your students will find that most people in advertising will have few problems in agreeing with James Bernardin. As the name of the Chapter implies, a good foundation is essential to a sound advertising program. As noted by Mr. Bernardin, the starting point for this foundation is homework. It brings order to originality, clarity to cleverness, and credibility to your creative product.

CHAPTER 6 - ADVERTISING COPYWRITING

6-1 In order to develop a Unique Selling Proposition, the advertiser should strive to create a proposition that the competition either cannot or does not offer. The proposition should also be strong enough to pull new customers to the product. Third, the proposition should offer a true proposition to the customer in the form of specific benefits. In terms of a USP for a chewing gum, the gum may have flouride in it, or be preferred by a particular reference group, or perhaps, be used to break the cigarette habit. Whatever is unique, has mass appeal, and represents a benefit will result in a USP for the chewing gum.

6-2 The Adoption Process consists of six stages:
  Awareness - Customer learns of product
  Interest - Customer searches for product information
  Evaluation - Customer has desire for product not yet bought
  Trial - Customer tries out product
  Adoption - Customer buys product
  Post Adoption - Customer rationalizes the adoption of the product.
The Adoption Process helps to explain how customers view a product. It also helps to explain what needs to be said to sell the product. In addition, the process points out the need to advertise to current customers as well as future ones. In advertising, never assume that customers cannot be found at all levels of the adoption process. Ads placed in the mass media should provide the necessary information for customers who may be found at any of the six stages of the adoption process.

6-3 A copy platform is needed for any advertising campaign. As the blueprint to be followed in creating the various ads for a campaign, it serves to summarize the various types of information that were obtained during the copy-thinking process. Not only should every campaign have a copy platform but it also should be written out in as detailed a form as possible. A well-planned copy platform is an effective tool of advertising development.

6-4 Some of the more popular advertising copy formats are:
  Testimonial - must appear to be believable
  Humorous - Be sure it is "funny"
  Cartoon - May lack credibility
  Straight-Sell - A positive ad that calls directly for action
  Slice-of-Life - A dramatization of a probable real life event, although
   many times presented as an exaggeration for impact purposes
  Verse - Promotes recognition by means of repetition
  News - Gives the impression that it is a news story
  Educational - Usually institutional in nature or may stress primary
   demand
  Combination of Formats - Combines the various formats for the purpose

of effectively presenting a message to a particular market
As examples of the different formats are given by the class, it should become
clear that most advertisements make use of more than one format. One format
may be predominate but others may be used. For example, the Igloo ad in the book
used a cartoon format to present a testimonial for the product.

6-5   All elements of copy structure are important but if the headline does not attract
the attention of the target audience, then no other part of the ad will matter
since it will not be seen or heard. Of course, once the headline has done its
job, other elements (body, close) become more important as the ad works to make
the sale. Copy structure strives to achieve the AIDA formula which calls for
Attention, Interest, Desire, Action. Attention (the headline) must come first
but the last element, Action (close) is what is required to justify the advertising
effort. In the final analysis, all elements of copy structure must be equally
important since all must be done well if the advertising program is to succeed.

6-6   The various types of headlines are:
        Stress Customer Benefits - 40 miles per gallon
        Arouse Curiosity - It can drive across the ocean
        Ask Questions - Does She or Doesn't She?
        Issue a Command - Don't buy a car - until you check with us
        Announce News - We have been selected as the number one television
            station in the state
        Attract Target Market - Hey teenager - Better listen!
Each type of headline serves to attract the attention of the target market by
various means. As a class assignment you could have your class bring in ads that
illustrate each of the six headline types as discussed in the book. There is,
of course, some overlap among types as the class exercise will serve to illustrate.

6-7   In closing an ad, things to consider are the selling approach and the passive
points. As for the selling approach, should hard sell or soft sell be used. The
hard sell approach calls for action now. It stresses that you should hurry and
buy while you can - don't procrastinate! Soft sell, on the other hand, is
designed to get action at some unknown future time when the need arises for the
product. Many national ads are of the soft-sell variety. Passive points is the
other important aspect of closing. Store name, address, credit options, and
copyright notices are all examples of passive points. When included, they may
not be noticed. When left out, they can become very important to the advertiser.

6-8   Words have no meaning. Only experience has meaning. Words used in an
advertisement will hopefully express what the advertiser wishes to say. The
copywriter will want to stay away from words with negative connotations such as
"death" or "loser." Positive words help to project a positive image for the
advertised item. As for message adaptation, improper English, slang, abbreviations,
and symbols of various kinds that are used by the target market may be used in the
advertisement as a means of "talking" the language of the market. The end result
may be an advertisement that the advertiser neither likes or understands. This
situation is no problem, so long as the same is not also true for the target market.
Rule number one of message adaptation, is "Know Thy Market."

6-9   The question will serve to reenforce the material presented in the Chapter. As
has been pointed out before, you might want to apply this question to a classroom
situation and bring the resource people to the classroom. Of course, there is
merit in having your students go to the outside people since it gives them a
chance to see a "live" agency and department in action.

6-10 (A) Unique Selling Proposition (USP) - The advertiser should attempt to develop a proposition that cannot be or is not used by competition which is strong enough to pull new customers to the product due to the buyer benefits that are expressed in the proposition.

(B) AIDA - Attention, Interest, Desire, Action - The good advertisement is developed with the AIDA formula in mind. As each part of the formula is achieved, the next element becomes the most important for the advertiser.

(C) KISS - Keep It Sweet and Simple or Keep It Simple Stupid. Simplicity is important in advertising. Don't write copy to impress. Write it so as to communicate. Simplicity is a function of the target market. Write copy so that it is easy for the market to absorb the advertising message.

(D) Gunning Fog Index - A system for measuring readability that penalizes the copywriter for using long sentences and polysyllabic words. Gives a close approximation of the educational grade level that a person would require to read and understand the particular written material.

CHAPTER 7 - ADVERTISING PRESENTATION

7-1 Balance is a layout principle that makes use of copy, illustration, and color to achieve a visual impression. The advertisement is divided into four quadrants with the optical center being 2/3 of the distance from the bottom of the ad or one third the distance above the measured center. It is this optical center where the eye will probably be drawn to an ad. In an ad with formal balance, layout elements are distributed equally on either side of the optical center. A layout of this type promotes a feeling of dignity, dependability, and security. For an ad that needs to be more creative, dynamic, and exciting, informal balance can be used. By using elements of different weight, an asymmetrical balance can be achieved as a large illustration on one side of the ad may be "balanced" by copy and color in another ad sector.

7-2 As a form of movement, indirect motion or gaze motion makes use of elements within the ad to make people "look" into the ad by the use of eyes, fingers, and other natural forms of motion. Although not structured, it can still direct a person through an ad if done properly. Numerous examples are available to illustrate this concept. Challenge your students to search out unusual examples of gaze motion.

7-3 Contrast strives to make the ad stand out so that it will be noticed by the target market. Unity strives to make all parts of the ad and, in turn, all ads work together. The two do not normally conflict with each other. Contrast works to achieve a distinction between the ads of the firm and competing firms but unity can still be present within the elements of the one campaign. Of course, taken to the extreme, contrast and unity could be in conflict if contrast is achieved at the expense of normally accepted standards of advertising development. Contrast, under such circumstances, may get attention, but will it sell the product? The advertiser should attempt to develop ads that consider both contrast and unity as copartners, not as adversaries.

7-4 The various stages of layout for print media are:
    Thought or Thumbnail Sketch - Rough sketch
    Rough Layout - Refined artwork - headline and copy placement is shown
    Comprehensive Layout - Detailed artwork - except for copy, resembles
        actual ad
    Mechanical Layout - Artwork and type in camera-ready form
    Actual Advertisement - taken from proof that is made from the mechanical

For television, the layout process makes use of a storyboard that may contain up to three elements (copy, visuals, and camera direction). As for radio, the well-planned script will include copy and sound directions. Point-of-purchase advertising as well as direct mail advertising will actually be created for study purposes. These layout ads are called dummys.

7-5 The layout of an ad is a key element in presenting the image of a product, store, and so forth. As discussed in the text, customers have learned what to expect in a discount store layout. If that type of ad layout is used, regardless of the copy or illustration, the image projected by the layout will be that of a discount or bargain operation. Every layout projects an image or a personality. The concern is whether it is projecting the appropriate image or personality.

7-6 The assignment as given may yield some good examples for your picture file for use in teaching future sections of advertising. Depending on the creativity of your class, the examples may prove to be quite interesting. Please stress to your students that they should not clip ads out of magazines in the University or College Library.

7-7 Line drawings have certain advantages over photographs. Some advantages are:
1. Because they are unique, they stand out from other illustrations.
2. They offer consistency of appearance when more than one product is shown in an ad.
3. They are easy to reproduce regardless of type of paper or process.
4. Black and white line drawings do not seem to suffer as much as black and white photographs in terms of impact.
5. They are cheaper (photo sessions, negative costs will be either eliminated or less expensive).
Examples of line drawings are more prevalent in business media. You might wish to direct your students to that media for their search for current examples.

7-8 Direct your students toward the various advertising and marketing journals as well as toward psychological publications. Have your students expand on the information that is presented in Figure 7-25. If library resources permit, expand the table to include information that would be helpful in the development of international advertising. The research exercise will serve to stress the point that color communicates.

7-9 Simply put - the answer is BOTH! If either is weak, the ad is weak. If both copy and artwork are strong, the ad should be strong.

7-10 This can be a fun exercise for the class. Select an unusual product. Some of the things I have used are chewing tobacco, solar-powered music box, cow moo noisemaker, and ballpoint pen with a light in the point. Select an unusual media - for example, Ladies Home Journal for the chewing tobacco ad. Now let the creative juices flow! Have all ads prepared on 8½" x 11" paper and then use an opaque projector to show various ones to the class for purposes of class discussion. Go over which format was used, how copy style could have been handled differently, the placement of the artwork, the use of gaze motion, etc. If you have never done this type of exercise before with a class, you may be surprised how creative your students can be. As noted earlier, this is a fun exercise but it is also a learning exercise. The student will use this ad to bring together the various points that have been discussed so far in the course. The various points should jell together as the ad is put together. It helps to do some advertising as a means of learning advertising.

LIBRARY
College of St. Francis
JOLIET, ILL.

CHAPTER 8 - ADVERTISING PRODUCTION

8-1   Letterpress - Printing from a raised surface.
         Lithography - Printing from a flat surface.
         Gravure - Printing from a recessed surface.
         Serigraphy - Printing by means of a stencil.

The most popular method of printing is probably Offset Lithography, which is now in use in most newspapers and many magazines. But each of the printing methods has its place. Letterpress Flexography is used to print packages and point-of-purchase paper displays. Direct Lithography is popular for printing outdoor posters. Gravure is used to print catalogs and other forms of direct mail advertising. Serigraphy is the choice for store window signs as well as for the imprinting of advertising messages on T-shirts. Which method of printing is best? It depends on the job to be done.

8-2   The different media use various reproduction techniques. Because of this, what the advertiser or production specialist needs to know is what form do the media want the ad to be in when it is submitted to the media. What type of screen does the media want used for the illustration? Will the media accept color? Is camera-ready copy required? Will the actual printing plate have to be supplied? Does the insertion deadline provide sufficient time to get the advertisement in the proper form? It is noted that many media will reject an ad that is submitted in the incorrect form. In many cases, it is just as easy to prepare the ad in the proper form as it is to do so incorrectly. Time and money can be saved by preparing all advertisements for insertion in the manner that is called for by the media.

8-3   Roman type - Makes use of serifs. Letters have variations in thickness in different parts of each letter. Gives a feeling of variety without changing type styles. Greatest strength is legibility. Good image.
Block type - May or may not have serifs. Thickness within each letter is uniform. Gives a modern, up-to-date image. Is not as easy to read as Roman type.
Script type - Looks like handwriting. Pure script gives the appearance of connected letters while cursive script is not connected in appearance. Projects an exclusive image but very difficult to read.
Ornamental type - All types not included in the first three categories are placed here. As for image or legibility, the type face will naturally determine these characteristics. No general statements can be made for this category.

8-4   Hot type is formed in hot metal that becomes part of a printing plate. Copy is usually created on a Monotype or Linotype machine for use in Letterpress printing. As for cold type, copy is "cast" on paper or film which is then transfered to a metal printing plate for printing purposes. Cold type printing is generally believed to be quicker cheaper, cleaner, and sharper than its hot-type counterpart. Most common application is Offset Lithography.

8-5   (A) Pica - A horizontal measure - 6 picas equal one inch.
        (B) Point - A vertical or height measure - 72 points equal one inch.
        (C) Agate Line - A vertical or height measure - 14 agates equal one inch depth by one column wide.
        (D) Lead - Spacing between lines (vertical) measured in points
        (E) Quad - Spacing between letters, columns, etc. (horizontal) measured in picas.
        (F) em - Space required to print the widest letter in the typeface (usually the M) in the type size being used. Usually measured in picas but may be measured in points.

LIBRARY

8-6   If the square-inch method of typefitting is used, the advertiser will count the total number of words in the copy and then divide this total by the number of words per square inch that can be set in the desired font. The answer will tell the advertiser how many square inches of layout space is needed in order to fit the copy into the print ad. Any example is possible. The one in the textbook uses 320 words set in 10 point type with a two point lead. Using the square-inch table in the book, there are 16 words per square inch for 10 on 12 type. Therefore, the copy requirement will call for 20 square inches of layout space.

8-7   The statement is incorrect. The selection of a screen size is a function of paper quality. The lower the quality of paper, the lower should be the screen number (larger the screen). An illustration using a fine screen would turn out a very poor reproduction on newsprint. However, a fine screen would be very desirable for printing on high quality paper.

8-8   Live-action and animation are two television production techniques. A live-action commercial uses real people and things in an ad. It can be produced live as well as on tape or film. Animation, on the other hand, involves the use of puppets, cartoons, and numerous tricks of the trade that can result in a car driving down the street by itself or a person sitting in a chair talking to his stomach sitting in the other chair. Due to its nature, it can't be done live, but film or videotape can be used. As for examples, the Levi commercials continue to be an excellent example of animation.

8-9   Once the shooting of the television commercial is complete, the first task is to create a rough cut (the best footage is spliced together so that the overall effect of the ad becomes evident). After the rough cut is deemed satisfactory the various optical effects (wipe, fade, etc.) are added and the sound is meshed with the visual portion of the ad. Upon completion of this task, the answer is now known about the quality of the ad. The answer print will then be shown to the client for approval.

8-10   By knowing something about advertising production, the advertiser should be better able to communicate what is desired and to understand the limitations of the various media. Better advertising can result if the advertiser has knowledge of the terminology and techniques of production.

CHAPTER 9 - MEDIA: AN OVERVIEW

9-1   In most areas, the list will include radio, newspaper, magazine, outdoor, directory, point-of-purchase, specialty, and television advertising. Some areas will also have transit and theater advertising. Many will overlook direct mail in this answer. Be sure to define the geographic area to be covered by the answer. Once the list has included the more common media, the list for any area may include shopping cart advertising, skywriting, advertisements projected on buildings, T-shirt ads, painted vehicles, and about anything else that may qualify in a given area. This question can be used as a brainstorming session. Why not try it and see just how many different advertising possibilities really do exist in your area.

9-2   Does a firm have as one of its objectives to promote a particular image? If so, the placement of ads in carefully selected media may help to foster that desired image. Also, certain media may be known as being more effective for generating sales leads. Such media (direct mail, television) may be selected for this purpose. If the objective is to create awareness, television with its mass audience may be the choice. There is little doubt that advertising objectives affect media selection. They should! The right ad in the right media should be a function of the goal or objective of the advertising program.

9-3   Cost should be viewed in two ways - out-of-pocket and cost-per-person. By looking at cost in both ways, the advertiser not only selects the most efficient (CPM) advertising buy but also one that can be paid for. The major television events during the year may yield very attractive CPM data but if the advertiser cannot afford the out-of-pocket outlay of $200,000+ for the ad, then it makes little difference that the ad has a desirable cost-per-thousand figure.

9-4   Selectivity is concerned with how well the media zeros in on the target market. Selectivity can be measured in terms of geography or demographics or some combination of the two. Newspapers typically concentrate on geographic selectivity while magazines aim at demographic groups. In larger markets, some media (radio, newspapers, magazines) may serve a particular geographic area on a demographically selected basis. The better the media selectivity matches the target market, the more efficient will be the media choice.

9-5   On the surface, the radio station appears to be a good advertising buy. Certainly, in terms of percentage of the market area, the circulation is high relative to the coverage area. However, before a sound determination is made about the worth of XPDQ, several things need to be known. Is the circulation/penetration figure a cumulative one or is it for a particular time of day? How many people in the target market listen to that station? It is possible that the target market could consist of 30,000 people, all of whom are in the 50,000 not included in the station's circulation figure. Finally, where did the circulation figure come from? Did it come from Arbitron or one of the other rating companies or did it come from the station itself? If it is an internal figure, there is always the possibility that the figure is subject to question.

9-6   They are equally important. In fact, they are interrelated. If a media restriction prohibits the advertising of a particular product in a particular media, then that media restriction makes that media unavailable to the advertiser. Availability is a two-step question. First, is the media vehicle itself available? Some areas, for example, do not have transit advertising. Second, if the media vehicle is available, then is the desired time or space available? If someone has already contracted for the back page of the media, then it is no longer available for others who want to use the same page. The space is not available. As for restrictions, it pays to know them from the beginning. If a particular magazine will not run a liquor ad, do not plan to place an ad for liquor in that publication. Prior knowledge of both media availability and media restrictions can help to save the advertiser time and money while working to reduce his/her frustration level.

9-7   How flexible are the media in your area? Have your students go to the media and determine from them their deadlines and other requirements. You might also have them go to major advertisers in order to get their reactions to what the media have told the students. Even within one media group, flexibility requirements will differ. The end product should be a list that can be given to all advertisers in the area for reference purposes.

9-8   Media support may improve the chances that the ad will be read, seen, or heard. The media can also help by providing the proper atmosphere for the ad. By selecting those media that reach the target market, the advertiser can "ride" these media into the minds of target customers. Anything that the media can do to enhance customer participation with the media, the greater the potential impact of placing advertisements in those media. Numerous examples which are similar to those in the book can be cited.

9-9 The discussion should reveal that such benefits do exist. Many are unwritten and some will not come to light unless a specific question is directed to a particular situation. Most students will react in a neutral way to this media characteristic. Students with business experience behind them, however, will usually react in a more positive manner to the question. Answers to this question will be hard to come by unless students really pursue the topic with the various advertising personnel.

9-10 It is very difficult to rank the characteristics in any order since all are important. In fact, the ones that may turn out to be important to a particular advertiser may be those characteristics that were ignored by that person. The fact that they were not considered made them important. Advertisers should weigh the fifteen characteristics very carefully in order to select that particular media mix that will carry the advertising message to the target market in the most efficient manner.

CHAPTER 10 - PUBLICATION MEDIA

10-1 Newspapers can be classified by:
Size/Format - papers are available in two sizes - standard and tabloid, with numerous formats. The goal of the industry is to move all papers into one of six different formats - most of which consist of 6 columns.
Frequency - daily (4 or more times a week), weekly (3 or less times a week), and as-needed are the three most common frequency intervals.
Content - news, gossip, entertainment, and business information are common content concentrations for newspapers.
Market Audience - geography, demographics, and any combination of the two may be the target audience for any given newspaper.
These various classifications are important to the advertiser because they assist in deciding on whether newspapers should be used in the media mix and if so, then what newspapers.

10-2 Retailers and other local business organizations have known for many years that one of the best ways to reach a local market is by means of the local newspaper. Most newspapers do offer geographic selectivity on a local level. Of course, some papers cover very wide areas and some offer certain types of demographic selectivity as well. Overall, for most newspapers circulation data and other information will support the contention that newspapers do offer geographic selectivity.

10-3 Disadvantages of newspapers from an advertising viewpoint include:
Lack of permanence - The average life of a newspaper ad is less than 24 hours for a daily newspaper - somewhat longer for a weekly newspaper. The advertiser should not expect the advertising impact to last very long after the insertion of a particular ad.
Poor Quality of Product - Newsprint is low quality, therefore the ads can be no better than the paper they are printed on. Most

papers also overflow with ads which results in a serious clutter problem. The ad must really be good to stand out from the crowd.

Limited Demographic Orientation - If the target market is tightly defined from a demographic standpoint, most papers that reach such a market will do so with much waste circulation. As noted in question 2, the strong suit for most newspapers is geographic selectivity, not demographic selectivity.

By comparing these ideas with advertisers, other problems may come to light which may be thought to be either general disadvantages or disadvantages that pertain to the particular local newspaper. Class discussion on this question will reveal what various advertisers had to say about using newspapers as an advertising vehicle.

10-4 Students should follow the general guidelines as presented in the text when analyzing preferred positions. The exercise should point out the great number of ads that are not put in a preferred position of any kind as well as the great number of ads that are competing with each other within a particular paper. For advertisers that did receive favorable positions, a check with the media and/or the advertiser will probably reveal that most such positions were not paid for by means of a preferred rate. Some were obtained by luck, but most were obtained by making a request with the insertion order. It will also probably be noted that certain advertisers seem to get more than their fair share of preferred positions. In this situation, media franchise is usually a factor. Direct your students' efforts toward such firms in order to ascertain, if possible, what those advertisers have done to receive the treatment that they receive from the media.

10-5 Combination Rate - When two or more papers are owned by the same company, the rate for placing the ad in all papers is cheaper than making separate buys for placing the ad in each of the papers.

Dual Rate - The local or retail rate is low in cost, allows for no commissions and is quoted in column inches. On the other hand, the national or general rate is more expensive, does permit commissions, and is quoted in agate lines. Most papers offer the dual rate structure with the local/retail rate being limited to local advertisers who sell to the ultimate consumer.

Milline Rate - Cost per agate line per one million circulation. A measure of relative comparison for newspapers.

Adjusted Milline Rate - The adjusted rate replaces total circulation with target market circulation. Provides a relative comparison of newspapers without the factor of waste circulation.

Hi-Fi Preprint - Usually printed in color on one side of a roll of newsprint with a repeating wallpaper pattern so that it can be cut at any point on the roll without a loss of advertising message. Spectra-Color preprint, on the other hand, has a fixed cutoff point which eliminates the need for a repeating effect.

10-6 Magazines can be classified by:

Size and Format - Pocket, standard, flat, and large. The most popular appears to be the flat size.

Frequency - Most common frequency is monthly, while the next most common interval is weekly.

Content/Market - Magazines can be classified into three groups - consumer, business, farm. Within each of the three groups are numerous further divisions by content and market.

10-7   Advantages of magazines include demographic selectivity (most magazines have a well-defined target market that may match up with the target market of the advertiser), permanence (people do not throw away magazines immediately), quality of workmanship (good paper and fine screens help to make ads turn out well), and editorial support (the specialized magazine can attract the specialized market to the ad and even give prestige to the ad due to its surroundings). As for disadvantages, lack of flexibility (magazines do not offer the option of last minute changes), limited availability (small markets, as well as restrictions, keep many advertisers from using magazines), and cost (an ad in a national publication may have a favorable CPM but the out-of-pocket requirement can be quite high) are all factors that must be considered by the potential magazine user. Do the advantages outweigh the disadvantages or vice versa? The answer obviously depends on the situation.

10-8   The statement is true - EVERYTHING ELSE BEING EQUAL. It is usually better to attempt to use the Adjusted CPM figure since it will compare rates based on the target market circulation. It is also important to know how the guaranteed circulation of the magazine compares with actual circulation. It is conceivable that the target market circulation could exceed the guaranteed circulation figure in an unusual set of circumstances, although such an occurrence is not likely. If it did happen, however, ACPM would be lower than CPM for the particular publication.

10-9   The best way to handle this question is to get the various reports from ABC and distribute them to your class. Such reports are available in quantity if your institution is a member of ABC ($5 a year - see Section I of Instructor's Manual). The students can see for themselves the various reports for both newspapers and magazines. As for audience measurements that relate product usage to audience, various private research firms such as Simmons Market Research Bureau have data available. Starch, Inra, Hooper is yet another firm that will correlate audience with product or demographics by type of magazine. A check of various research directories will provide the names of firms and the types of information that may be available on the audience for print media.

10-10 The student can update the tables of users in the book if Advertising Age is available. In addition, a check of the media will reveal that usage of print media is quite high. The question as stated is open-ended in nature. The exercise should illustrate to the student that organizations of all types use print media in numerous ways. You should emphasize to your students that the applications are numerous. Therefore, no advertiser should automatically rule out the use of publication media in the media mix. Instead, a careful analysis should be made of how publication media might be used. If further analysis indicates that this type of media is not viable, then a judgment can be made that will eliminate publication media from the mix. It is important to emphasize that to not use publication media is fine, but only after a study has been made of that option. Naturally, the same holds true for all media.

CHAPTER 11 - BROADCAST MEDIA

11-1   Signal behavior and type of station can have a bearing on whether the target market receives the advertising message. In terms of signal behavior, physical barriers in the signal area can affect the performance of the FM (straight-line) signal. Tall buildings and other obstructions can cause the FM signal to break up. If this happens, the effect of the media is diminished. On the other hand, the AM signal will not be as static-free as the FM signal but it will carry better, especially in the evening hours if signal strength is not reduced. As for type of station, the target audience of the station, programming format, and programming sources will, hopefully, work together to reach the desired target market. A station that puts together the appropriate mix of the variables should attract the desired target market as its audience - the goal of any advertising vehicle.

11-2 Advantages of radio include geographic and demographic selectivity (most stations serve a demographic group within a geographic signal area), flexibility (short notice is the normal requirement for insertions or changes), and cost (local radio in many markets is the cheapest available media). As for disadvantages, these include perishability (once placed on the air, it is gone), clutter (numerous ads are run back to back), lack of visual support (can't show it on radio), and background medium (many people don't really listen to radio in the same way that they concentrate on a magazine or on television).

11-3 If rating service data are available, compare the results with what the stations indicate are their markets, formats and programming sources. For purposes of discussion, have the class first determine among themselves what audience each station supposedly is reaching. Their perceived image of each station will probably not match in all cases with either what the station says that it does or what the ratings indicate. When the analysis is complete, you might ask the class which stations a particular advertiser might choose for advertising purposes. Examples could be a car dealer, tractor dealer, soft drink bottler, bank, and so forth. Students will probably begin to request more information about each advertiser before a decision is made. If so, the assignment is a success. The advertiser needs to know the target market before media selection is possible.

11-4 Arbitron uses a diary which has the respondent write down when the radio is on and what it was tuned to. Pulse, on the other hand, collects data by means of a personal interview that asks the respondent what they listened to yesterday. Each system has its followers. As to which one the students prefer, you might wish to poll the class. You might also ask them to give their views on coincidental surveys as well. The best answer may be to use all methods to overcome the problems inherent in any of the measurement methods if funds and time permit.

11-5 One hundred gross rating points equals the number of ad impressions that is equivalent to the total population of the market area. Note that a 100 GRP does not mean that the ad reached 100 percent of the population. Some were exposed to the ad more than once. Such frequency is usually thought to be desirable. If only 50 percent of the population saw the ad but each of that 50 percent saw the ad twice, then the ad would have an audience rating that would be equivalent to 100 GRP's. As noted in the chapter, the GRP calculation can be used to determine the potential impact of a given radio package. Also, as will be noted in a later chapter, GRP is used to measure the impressions that will be received in an outdoor poster campaign. As an audience measurement, GRP's are being used more and more by ad buyer and seller alike.

11-6 The national advertiser may buy time on the CBS Evening News so that the ad will be aimed to all homes watching the news. If this approach will not give the desired level of coverage, the advertiser may, instead, choose the spot market where the national advertiser buys time on selected stations - not a network. Spot advertising allows the advertiser to take careful aim at the target market by carefully selecting the stations to be used. Affiliates from all the networks may be selected as well as independents. It is also possible that more than one station in an ADI may be used. Needless to say, network advertising and spot advertising are not terms for the same thing unless a general statement is made to the effect that they are both types of broadcast advertising.

11-7   If Advertising Age, The Wall Street Journal, Broadcasting and other similar sources are available, the results of this assignment could be a very complete study of the evaluation of cable television. The growth of the Super Station as well as the two-way cable system which permits viewer feedback should be included in the study along with the various "networks" that have been created to serve the many cable systems. Cable television is destined to have a growing impact on television in the years to come. By conducting this study of its evolution, your students will have a better understanding of an area that will have a growing impact on television and advertising in the foreseeable future.

11-8   An ADI (Area of Dominant Influence) is a geographic market design that defines one television market to the exclusion of another by means of measureable viewing patterns. All advertisers should find the ADI data to be of interest. If an advertiser wishes to reach certain counties by means of television, it is possible to determine which stations serve that area best in terms of viewing patterns. It is a useful tool for media selection.

11-9   The survey will usually reveal that consumers perceive that clutter is a problem. Such findings will reenforce the conclusions of the Marketing Service Institute and ANA study which indicate that clutter hurts advertising effectiveness.

11-10   The purpose of the question is to emphasize to the student that television may be great for many products but it is also expensive. Prime time television will probably be higher than it was when the book was published as will most other television rates. Ask your students how much advertising in other media could be bought for the money spent on that prime time ad or for that ad on the Super Bowl or other major television event. Even local rates should be enlightening to your beginning advertising students. As the rates are discussed, remind your students what they are buying (the ability to show and tell, geographic selectivity, and market penetration, along with ad clutter, and perishability). Does television cost too much? To some, the answer is "yes." Not every advertiser can afford the dollars required to reach 70 million viewers with a single ad. For others who do not need to reach such a mass market, the answer is also "Yes." For this group, there are probably other media that can do the job more efficiently.

CHAPTER 12 - DIRECT MEDIA

12-1   Direct Mail Advertising - This includes all forms of mailed direct advertising, except mail order. Its purpose may be to arouse interest, to assist in buying, or to familiarize prospects with the name of the product, its maker, its merits, and its distributors.
        Mail Order Advertising - This will do all that direct mail advertising will do and then will attempt to close the sale. It is responsible for the entire selling job.
        Direct Advertising - Since the above two terms are types of direct advertising, the definition of direct advertising is also needed. It is defined as advertising messages that are in some written, printed, or processed form which are sent by controlled circulation direct to selected individuals.
        Direct Marketing - A marketing system that offers products and services to present and potential customers and prospects through the use of various promotional

media, singly or in combination, to effect a direct action response by mail, telephone, or personal visit.

From the definitions, it is noted that direct marketing is not limited to the mail as a delivery vehicle and that it could involve direct contact with the customer. Mail order advertising does not involve personal contact as it makes the sale, whereas direct mail advertising may not have as its objective to close a sale, only to inform or assist in some way. Needless to say, there is much overlap in meaning among the various terms.

12-2   There are numerous forms of direct mail that an advertiser might use. Some of the more common ones are:

Letters - whether fancy or simple, computerized or printed, personalized or nonpersonal, letters can be very effective. As the most popular form of direct mail, a well-prepared letter can be very effective in the promotion of most products, services, and/or ideas.

Postcards - may be used to solicit business or can be used as the means for the customer to respond to the mailing.

Booklets - may be used to present an in-depth sales story.

Broadside - size is its greatest benefit. The impact of the bed sheet when unfolded can be very effective.

Brochures - typically a one-page selling tool that is folded to give several "pages" of copy. Not as elaborate as a booklet or as inexpensive as a circular. Very popular direct advertising tool.

Circulars - sometimes called a throwaway, this low cost advertising vehicle is often printed on newsprint.

Catalogs - a very expensive sales tool that is designed as a long-life promotional device.

Stuffers - designed to be sent piggyback style with the monthly statement or other mail pieces. Stuffers may attempt to solicit an order or just create interest.

12-3   Direct mail is thought to have both advantages and disadvantages. Points in favor of direct mail are permanence (piece can be read over and over again if customer wishes to do so), flexibility (postal regulations and budgetary restraints are about the only things that limit flexibility), impact (when received, there is little to distract the customer), selectivity (direct mail can zero in on prospects, not suspects), and measurability (by counting responses, it is easy to measure the results of direct response direct mail). On the negative side, disadvantages of direct mail are thought to include cost (postage, printing, names, and returns can add up to a very expensive promotion), lack of editorial support (must recruit its own audience), and lack of reader interest (many people view direct mail as junk mail). As is true with most media, people within the advertising industry will not always agree with all the advantages and/or disadvantages as listed. As a class exercise, you might wish to ask your students to add to the lists any advantages or disadvantages that they feel merit the attention of the advertiser.

12-4   A very important ingredient in successful direct mail marketing is sending the mail piece to the prospect, instead of a suspect. Most "occupant" mailings are sent to everyone in a particular zipcode area or to some other geographic zone. Even if the person receiving the mail piece is a prospect, what impact does the mail piece have when it is addressed in this nonpersonal manner? Most people love to see their name. Most people like to feel that the mail that is sent to them is for them. "Occupant" strikes out on both counts. Postal patron, boxholder, occupant, resident, and other similar terms do not have a place in a well-planned direct mail promotion.

12-5 Compiled lists contain the names and addresses of people who can be categorized in a meaningful way because they <u>are</u> something (college students, Catholics, live in Washington, D.C., and so on). Rented lists, on the other hand, refer to lists of names and addresses of people who <u>have done</u> something (obtained a Visa card, subscribed to <u>Good Housekeeping</u>, bought merchandise from Horchow, and so on). Which is better? The answer depends on the type of names that are needed. If geography or demographics is desired, a compiled list is the choice. If a list is desired that only includes names of people who have bought by mail within the last two years, then a search will need to be made for the appropriate rented list.

12-6 The best time of the year to send out a direct mail piece is January in terms of expected mail order response. Also, the latter part of the year, taken as a group, is more effective than the first part of the year. As for the best potential direct mail customer, that person will tend to be older (over 35), live in rural areas, and have bought by mail before.

12-7 Depending on your location, this question may or may not be realistic. In many areas, the only mail pieces being used are letters mailed in #10 envelopes. No experimentation has been attempted in terms of trying to see what pulled best. If such is the case, you may direct your students to present the various options to the business person so as to get his/her opinion as to which one might work better. This exercise could result in some business firms trying some of the ideas as presented.

12-8 Attempt to ascertain if consumers in your area are aware of computer letters or do they believe that such letters are really personal in nature. If they are aware of computer letters, does the effectiveness appear to suffer? Does the use of the person's name in the body of the letter help readership? Does the use of jet printing and other printing techniques that do not look like typewriting help or hurt a letter? Some major advertisers have had good results with computer letters. It should be interesting to learn what consumers in your area think about them. The information collected could be of assistance to the businesses who serve the area.

12-9 The purpose of this question is to get the student to give some thought to the break-even procedure as presented in the text and given in Figure 12-8. The procedure as given is a very complete yet easy way to consider all costs of a direct mail promotion for any type of firm. This one topic alone makes the book worth keeping for those students who will ever attempt to plan a direct mail promotion. From first hand experience, the procedure has proven itself in several businesses where I have been involved as a consultant. Break-even analysis is a very effective planning tool for direct mail.

12-10 As an alternative to this question, you might put several direct mail pieces on reserve in your library and have all students evaluate the same mail pieces by checking them out of the library. The evaluation should stress how the mail piece appeals to the target market, how it presents its sales message, how it uses various techniques to accomplish its objective, and so on. The student's mail piece should be presented in ready-to-mail form. If you wish to be strict with the assignment, you might check the current postal regulations to see if the mail pieces could be mailed and if yes, at what rate. Once again, an alternative to the question is to assign a product so that all mail pieces can be compared. Encourage creativity. The assignment usually results in many mail pieces, some that are not practical for a realistic budget and several that are very good.

It can be a beneficial learning experience for your students if time will permit you to discuss the completed mail pieces in class.

CHAPTER 13 - MOBILE MEDIA

13-1   Mobile media (out-of-home media) consist of outdoor and transit advertising. All forms of mobile media try to "drive" home the message to the customer while the customer is not at home. Being a supportive media, almost any type of product, service, or idea has been promoted by means of mobile media. Firms with particular interest in this media are businesses that sell to the traveling public (airlines, motels, restaurants).

13-2   The Outdoor Advertising Association of America has set particular standards for outdoor signs such as all frames for posters will be 22 feet 8 inches by 10 feet 5 inches. Standardized media include all posters and bulletins as discussed in question 13-3. Nonstandardized media include roadside signs (nonconforming, custom-built posters and bulletins), on-premise signs (business sign on the grounds of the business - Holiday Inn sign), and spectaculars (custom-built sign consisting of flashing lights, three dimensional components, electronic message boards, and so on which is placed at a high traffic location such as along side a main city expressway or Times Square).

13-3   A poster consists of sheets of paper that are printed, taken to the site, and then glued to the board. All posters fit into the same frame (22 feet 8 inches by 10 feet by 5 inches). Three types of posters are 24-sheet, 30-sheet, and bleed.
>   24-sheet - Usually printed on ten sheets. "Live" advertising area is 19 feet 6 inches by 8 feet 8 inches.
>   30-sheet - Usually printed on fourteen sheets. Copy area is 21 feet 7 inches by 9 feet 7 inches. Provides 25 percent more space for copy than the 24-sheet poster.
>   Bleed - Provides 40 percent more copy area than the 24-sheet poster. No blanking is used. Copy area is same as frame area (22 feet 8 inches by 10 feet 5 inches).

A bulletin contains approximately three times as much square footage of advertising space as a poster. Its size (48 feet by 14 feet) gives impact to an advertising message. Bulletins are normally painted at the outdoor company and then transported to the site for installation. Two special types of bulletins are available - embellished bulletin and trivision bulletin.
>   Embellished Bulletin - Has extensions that project outside the standard bulletin. According to industry standards, the extensions may not extend over 5 feet 6 inches above the board or 2 feet on either side or the bottom of the bulletin. Sometimes referred to as a 3-D Bulletin because of the effect that is presented.
>   Trivision Bulletin - May contain up to three different advertising messages. Board will rotate to show another message every few seconds. Rate of rotation depends on traffic flow. If a three-part message for the same advertiser is used, the full impact of the bulletin may not be possible for fast-moving traffic. All bulletin locations are not conducive to Trivision applications.

In regard to examples, the exercise will stimulate your students to look at outdoor advertising. If your area is like most, it will not be difficult for your students to find bad examples to go along with some good examples of outdoor advertising.

13-4   The Traffic Audit Bureau (TAB) provides an impartial source for circulation data for outdoor in much the same way that ABC does for print media. Such data is derived from both machine and hand counts. In addition to traffic counts, Audience Market by Market for Outdoor (AMMO) audience data provides information for many markets regarding how many and what kind of people can be reached with outdoor advertising. Have your students see if AMMO is available in your area. Do advertisers understand it? In many cases, the answer will be "No." As you probably are already aware, some outdoor companies have little or no audience data while others, who are usually active in the Outdoor Association, will provide the advertiser as well as your students with TAB, AMMO, and surveys, studies, and so on that deal with audience data. The amount of available information will definitely vary from market to market.

13-5   When "buying" posters, the typical buy will consist of a set number of posters that will be placed throughout the market area so that a particular GRP will be achieved. Both reach and frequency will normally be high. In one study cited in the book, 89.2 percent of total adults were reached in 30 days in an average market with a frequency rate of 31 times. AMMO data should also be used, if available. The minimum buy for outdoor is normally one month with all artwork, printing, etc. in addition to the rental fee. It is recommended that the advertiser "ride a showing" to see exactly where each poster will be placed since such an activity may result in better locations being used for the ad. In addition to the above considerations, the advertiser should consider if it is appropriate to advertise image-wise by means of outdoor and whether the target market could be reached more efficiently in other media. These last considerations obviously hold true for bulletins as well as posters. As for bulletins, the traffic count at the particular site of the bulletin is crucial as well as the demographics of the people passing the site. Is the site considered to be a preferred location? As for cost, the bulletin is usually purchased for a period of one year with or without a rotary plan which would move the bulletin from location to location during the year. Production costs are also quite high for bulletins but their impact due to size makes them a viable option for many advertisers.

13-6   For outdoor advertising, advantages include reach and frequency (high repetition of a 100 GRP buy promotes recall), market selectivity (ad placements can be tailored to the customer), cost (usually has attractive out-of-pocket and CPM cost figures), and size (large size helps to get attention). As for disadvantages, brevity (must get the message across quickly), image (doesn't project an exclusive image), clutter (many signs find themselves surrounded by numerous distractions), and location choices (good locations are often not available) are problems for the outdoor user. In regard to transit media, overall advantages include cost (offers an attractive CPM as well as out-of-pocket figure) and reach and frequency (the same people ride the bus often or see it often). Advantages specifically related to car cards are that they provide a chance to sell the customer as he/she goes to town and they give impact. The whole inside of the bus may carry ads for just one product. As for exterior displays, geographic selectivity is a plus as is impact. A total bus will only carry ads for one advertiser on the exterior of the vehicle. As it goes to a particular part of town where the target market is located, the vehicle should receive many favorable ad impressions. Like outdoor, transit advertising also has certain disadvantages. These include limited demographic selectivity (many transit situations are only suitable for mass appeal), limited availability (small-town America has no transit advertising), and image (clutter and confusion is the common environment for much transit advertising). When comparing the two media types, cost, reach and frequency, and impact are pluses for both outdoor and transit advertising while a common disadvantage is believed to be image.

13-7 A 100 showing yields an exposure level that is equal to 100 percent of the mobile population of the area in a 30-day period. A 100 GRP means that the ad exposure level would equal 100 percent of the population, not that the ad has been exposed to everyone in the population. A GRP calculation tends to be less subjective than the calculations for a showing. Showing calculations are still used by some outdoor companies and for certain types of transit media. GRP is becoming a common method for measuring ad impressions.

13-8 There are three types of transit media: car cards, exterior displays, and station displays. Car cards are located inside transit vehicles, usually in buses. The standard car card is 11 inches high and either 21, 28, 42, or 56 inches long. Exterior displays are located on the outside of transit vehicles (buses, taxis). Standard exterior displays include the king-size poster (30 inches by 144 inches), headlight display (21 inches by 44 inches), and traveling spectacular (16½ inches by 36 inches). Station displays may be found in terminals and similar environments. Exhibits, posters, and moving signs are three common examples. As for how the cost is figured for each type of transit advertising, the quoted figure is a rental fee for space. Production cost for the ad is a separate expense. Also, most transit advertising is purchased for a 30-day period. As for cost in terms of audience exposure, the transit industry lacks the hard audience data that is available for other media. Car cards are purchased by service value, exterior displays by showing, and station displays by intensive, representative, or minimum showing. For each transit company, the advertiser must ask that company to define what is meant by the terms used and what are the sources for the data. As noted in question 13-6, transit advertising is inexpensive as compared to other media. A careful analysis of the audience reached should be made to insure that the relatively small amount spent on transit advertising does not turn out to be wasted dollars.

13-9 Moods-In-Motion - A trade name used by a transit advertising firm which means the same thing as a basic bus (all advertisements placed inside a bus are for the same company or product).
Total-Total Bus - All advertisements placed inside and outside the bus are for the same company or product.
Take-One Card - A special type of car card which offers the advertiser the opportunity to use direct response advertising in conjunction with transit media.
TAB - The Traffic Audit Bureau provides an impartial source of circulation data for outdoor media.
Rotary Plan - A plan whereby an advertiser purchases a bulletin that will be moved to a different location each month or at some other predetermined time interval. The rotary plan should promote greater reach. A popular variation of the rotary plan is for the advertiser to acquire three bulletins which are then rotated over time at the three sites. This plan gives variety while improving both reach and frequency.
Service Values - A means of measuring transit advertising circulation for car cards. Full service value, half service, etc., will yield potential exposures equal to a figure as defined by the individual transit company.

13-10 Major users of outdoor advertising include the makers of cigarettes and liquor along with those who serve the traveling public. As for transit advertising, mass appeal products such as soft drinks and chewing gum are heavy users. For local transit users, use is a function of the type of transit system and who uses it.

When your students discuss the use of mobile media with users in your area, the most common reason that will probably be given for use is cost. The exercise should illustrate to your students that many advertisers have not given much thought as to why they are using mobile media. You might ask your class the question – Should cost be the primary reason for using any media? Cost is, of course, a factor but it should not be the only one when deciding on the use of media.

CHAPTER 14 – POINT-OF-PURCHASE MEDIA AND OTHER MEDIA

14-1   Types of Point-of-Purchase advertising include:

On-premise signs – primary function is business identification.

Window displays – may be promotional (sell the product), institutional (sell the firm), or public service (sell the Girl Scouts).

Wall displays – semi-permanent in nature. Common for promoting beer and soft drink brands.

Cutouts – short-life expectancy display usually made of cardboard or a similar product. May consist of the shipping carton with the top cut in a particular way for display purposes.

Merchandise racks – may be permanent or disposable. Takes the product out of its ordinary environment so that it will stand out from competing products.

Display cards – message quality and physical quality of the display card are both crucial to point-of-purchase effectiveness.

Audiovisual displays – effectiveness is diminished if other similar displays are present.

Vending machines – they not only advertise the product, they also attempt to complete the sale.

Product itself – whether showing the actual product (new car) or its package (cereal), the product itself can be a very effective tool in helping the customer decide to buy the product.

Good and bad examples of point-of-purchase advertising are usually not hard to find. A visit to most food stores, for example, will yield some of each. Some of the poor examples will probably be displays with messy "hand-printed" display cards, ones that make the customer feel unsafe, and ones that make it difficult for customers to actually take the product from the display. Good examples, on the other hand, will usually consist of those point-of-purchase displays that push the product instead of themselves.

14-2   Point-of-purchase advertising has the following advantages: promotes impulse buying (point-of-purchase advertising helps people see the product), reenforces other promotional efforts (can remind people that they have seen previous ads for the product), and sells in self-service environment (when no salesperon is there, the only "salesperson" is a point-of-purchase display). As for disadvantages, these include design (should not be too creative; good displays sell products, not displays), placement (a good display must be seen to be effective), and clutter (the typical store contains numerous point-of-purchase displays). The discussion with users of point-of-purchase advertising in your area should yield responses very similar to what is given in the text. The main purpose in asking your students to go to users is that it will get your students to look at numerous point-of-purchase displays in use. If answered concurrently, this exercise will also assist the student in answering question 14-1.

14-3   As presented by Orville Ottow, the four I's of Point-of-Purchase Advertising are:
        Impact - P-O-P should attract the attention of the customer and then turn
            that attention into interest.
        Identification - P-O-P should tell who/what the company/product is.
        Information - P-O-P should tell the customer what she/he needs to know
            in terms of product knowledge.
        Imagery - P-O-P tells the customer that the product is relevant along
            with the idea to "buy me."
        Every good point-of-purchase display should strive to meet the requirements for
        each of the four I's.

14-4   Some people feel that specialty advertising is only useful as a gimmick device.
        Others who understand the medium realize that specialty advertising encompasses
        many items (over 30,000) for numerous purposes (advertising specialties, advertising
        calendars, business gifts) whose advantages include long life, flexibility, and
        selectivity. With annual sales for the specialty industry now being in the
        neighborhood of $3 billion, the days of viewing the specialty industry as just
        a gimmick media are past. In its place is an industry that concentrates on
        selling to advertisers useful items of merchandise that are imprinted with the
        advertiser's name or logo and that are distributed without obligation to customers
        and prospects. Either standing alone or being supportive of the other elements in
        the media mix, specialty advertising is a media alternative that should be
        analyzed by every advertiser.

14-5   In figure 14-5, the Specialty Advertising Association International lists 17
        situations where specialty advertising can be used. You might select one or
        several of the choices given and have your students present in detail how they
        would use specialty advertising to serve the specific specialty application(s).
        If the question is answered in total as given in the book, you might ask your
        students to expand on the list. Everything from a political candidate to the
        U.S. Army can be promoted by means of a key chain or other specialty advertising
        item. The greatest benefit to your students of this exercise is that it should
        make it clear that specialty advertising does have many possible uses in the
        media mix.

14-6   From an advertising standpoint, an organization should place an advertisement in
        a directory if the directory in question fills a need and is available to those
        who might need it. Of course, the assumption is that those who need the
        particular directory are found to be in the firm's target market. The latter part
        of the exercise will point out to the student that there are numerous directories
        in addition to the Yellow Pages and that most directories are found in the
        business sector of the market. As a class assignment, you might wish to divide
        your class up by industry type and have them go to different firms and ask them
        what directories are available for their business types. Once the field work is
        done, a composite list from all sampled industries should be quite extensive.

14-7   Theatrical advertising is advertising in a movie theater. Impact due to screen
        size and geographic/demographic selectivity are points in favor of this media.
        The media does not, however, reach all markets in the United States since many
        people do not go to the movie theater. As you will note in Advertising Age, one
        theater advertising company, Screenvision, is promoting itself to advertisers as
        a media alternative. Screenvision has been successful in Europe and is now
        attempting to achieve this same success in the United States market. As for
        nontheatrical advertising, this form of "advertising" involves making a movie
        about something which will use the company or products or both as the vehicle to

tell the story. Because of its institutional nature, the impact of nontheatrical advertising is hard to measure. Certainly, no short-term impact on sales should be expected from this method of "advertising."

14-8   "Never" is a very strong statement when talking about donation advertising but "never" is correct if it is to be charged to the advertising budget. Donation advertising should be charged to the goodwill or public relations budget but never to the advertising budget since its primary purpose is not to inform, persuade, or sell the target market. The smart advertiser will attempt to avoid such ad placements. When this is not possible, camera-ready copy (slick) should be given to the organization so that the advertisement that is given as a donation will at least have the name of the advertiser spelled correctly.

14-9   A question of this type was asked in Chapter 9. Now that the more popular media choices have been discussed and questions along the way have brought your students and advertisers/agencies together, it should be interesting to see if the media choices as given in Chapter 9 can now be expanded. Of course, if you did not assign question 9-1, this will be your students' first effort at such a list. If so, the purpose of the exercise will be to point out to your students that media choices are numerous. It is suggested that you discuss this question in class so that a master list can be developed. The list could prove helpful to your students at some future time in their career.

14-10   Most students will probably select either newspapers or television as the most important media while transit, specialty, or theatrical are some of the media that may be chosen to head the list of least important. After hearing the discussion, emphasize that the most or least important media choice really depends on the client and the job to be done by the media. The media that will deliver the message in the most effective manner to the target market is the most important media for that client for that particular situation. The same type of reasoning is true as well for the least important media.

CHAPTER 15 - ADVERTISING BUDGET

15-1   Distinguish between these terms:
        Advertising appropriation - the lump sum figure that the firm will spend
            on advertising.
        Advertising budget - a detailed advertising plan that deals with how the
            advertising appropriation will be spent.
        Budget attrition - the inclusion of nonadvertising items in the advertising
            budget or advertising allocation.
        Advertising allocation - in budgeting, the division of funds according to
            time, geography, product and service, and/or other considerations.
        The advertiser should follow the cycle where appropriation leads to budget which leads to allocation. At each point in the process, care should be taken to insure that only advertising expenses are charged to the advertising account. If other expenses are permitted in the advertising budget, it becomes very difficult to evaluate the true advertising effort from a dollar standpoint.

15-2   A budget for advertising makes sense. Why? Because the budget procedure forces planning. Because it provides accountability by stipulating where the money will be spent and, consequently, who is accountable for that expenditure. Because it promotes efficiency which results from the coordination that both planning and accountability encourage by their nature.

15-3   There is nothing wrong with using the percentage-of-sales method for determining
        the advertising appropriation. The problem occurs when it is the only method
        that is used. As a method, it is probably the most popular technique in use
        due to its simplicity. The difficulty with the method stems from the dilemma of
        which comes first - advertising or sales - and whether last year's sales should
        determine this year's advertising budget. When used in conjunction with other
        methods (market-share, competitive-parity, task, and so on) and with judgment,
        the percentage-of-sales method can play a role in the development of an
        appropriate advertising appropriation for the firm.

15-4   The competitive-parity method of determining the advertising appropriation calls
        for the advertiser to set an amount for advertising that is equivalent to what
        the competition is spending. It is noted that followship can be dangerous. Is
        it correct to assume that the competition knows what they are doing? Also, in
        most cases, competitive-parity must be based on historical data since current
        data will not be available from trade associations and other similar sources. As
        for the all-you-can-afford method, the procedure seems logical since the firm will
        never place itself in financial jeopardy by spending too much on advertising
        or hurt itself in the market by advertising too little. The greatest problem
        with this subjective approach is the question of what can the firm really
        afford and whether the level of advertising is what is needed by the firm. The
        all-you-can-afford method can result in too much or too little being spent on
        advertising when used by itself to determine the appropriation. The two methods
        as given are very popular with both large and small firms. Small firms, in
        particular, like the competitive-parity method. Some will carry this approach
        to the extreme by running an ad to match every ad run by the competition. This
        eye-for-an-eye technique is very popular with media salespeople, particularly
        when they can find two competitors who try to match each other.

15-5   As observed by J. O. Peckham of the A. C. Nielsen Company, there does appear to
        be a relationship between market share and share of advertising. If a firm
        wishes to maintain or increase market share, the advertising share should equal
        or exceed the share of the market. For new products, advertising share should
        double expected market share. For example, if sales for the left-handed widget
        industry are projected to be $100 million, total advertising expenditures for
        the industry are $14 million, and projected market share for the firm is 25
        percent or $25 million in sales; then the firm's projected advertising
        appropriation would be $7 million or 50 percent of industry advertising share.
        As for the task method, the procedure calls for the firm to determine objectives
        or stated tasks and then determine what it will cost to accomplish the stated
        advertising objectives. This technique builds a budget based on objectives. The
        need is first determined, then funded. Most other methods simply determine how
        much money is available. These other approaches rarely find any money left over
        even when the approach used results in an excess amount being appropriated. As
        an example, the firm may determine that the objective is to increase sales by
        6 percent by working to generate sales leads in several clearly-defined target
        markets. Since the advertiser now knows what needs to be done, the appropriation
        can be designed with the specific task in mind. When the two approaches are
        compared, the task method is probably the more desirable since it puts planning
        in the proper sequence. As for the market-share method, the relationship between
        the variables is apparent and, therefore, useful but such a method ignores
        factors such as the quality of the advertising. Like all methods, both market-
        share and task are important and should be considered when the advertiser is
        involved in the process of determining the advertising appropriation.

15-6   The question will reveal to your students that most firms (small) do not make an effort to determine what the appropriation should be. Those who use any method at all will use the percentage-of-sales technique. Of course, some of the larger firms and some agencies will provide insight into how the budgeting process should be done as they explain how they determine the appropriation by both qualitative and quantitative methods. Perhaps of greatest interest to your students will be the fact that even the more sophisticated procedures in use still utilize subjective techniques. Judgment is a vital ingredient in any procedure for determining the advertising appropriation.

15-7   Although published in 1960, the list as presented in Printers' Ink is not significantly different from what is true today. Of course, the interpretation of certain items on the list may have changed in the time interval. For example, space and time cost in regular media may now include cable television advertising as well as the placement of ads in electronic newspapers or magazines. The list may also differ for different types of businesses. For example, point-of-sale materials and window display installation costs may be much higher on the list for particular retail stores. For others, these costs would be found in the No section of the list. The purpose of the exercise is to develop a working knowledge of what should or should not be charged to the advertising budget. The exercise should help to emphasize the problems that are inherent in budget attrition.

15-8   Factors that influence the size of the advertising budget are:
      Product Life Cycle - A product in the introductory stage will require more money for advertising than a product in the latter stages of the cycle.
      Competition - Active competition may result in a larger advertising budget. Followship is not implied in the factor but competition cannot be ignored.
      Promotional Strategy - the promotional mix which is made up of personal selling, advertising, publicity, and sales promotion, will influence the budget as will the choice of strategy (pull vs. push, etc.).
      Uncontrollable External Restraints - Economic, legal, and customer problems may all necessitate unexpected expenditures or dictate a drop in the budgetary needs of the firm. In a time of recession, the firm may have less need to advertise, therefore a smaller budget will be required. It is noted that some advertising is recommended in order to maintain the cumulative impact of advertising in the market place.

As for the last part of the question, almost any thing might be listed for a given firm. One that could be listed is the financial position of the firm. If the firm has limited funds available, the size of the appropriation and the budget will be influenced by this fact.

15-9   Although not permitted by the IRS to be treated as a capital expenditure, advertising should be viewed as a long-term capital investment on the basis of the cumulative effect that results from running advertising over time. Current advertisements have more clout because of past advertisements. Long-term planning for advertising which should result in continuity over time as well as desired levels of reach and frequency on a continuing basis is intelligent marketing. For the 500 word essay, you might look for the points expressed above. For further information, you might direct your students to note 18 in the chapter as well as to other sources that examine this topic area.

15-10   The first thing the student needs to know is the objectives of the firm. Does the firm wish to increase market share? With approximately 10 percent of the market, while advertising expenditures represent only 4 percent, there is apparent growth potential if advertising expenditures are increased to a level more closely approximating market share. This assumes that market share has historically exceeded advertising share as opposed to this being a one time phenomenon. Beyond these observations, the student can assume various types of information in order to apply the various qualitative and quantitative methods for determining the advertising appropriation. By making further assumptions, the budget can be derived and appropriate allocations made by time, geography, and so on. The exercise serves to bring together the various elements of budgeting as presented in the chapter. As a class discussion question, this question can be very helpful in pointing out that there are numerous ways to derive a budget and that the decision as to which way is best is partly subjective in nature.

CHAPTER 16 - MEDIA PLAN

16-1   Factors that can have a bearing on the media plan are:
   Size of Advertising Budget - The media plan must be made within the constraints of the budget.
   Media Discount Structure - Discount structures do affect media choice. In some cases, slight changes in the media plan due to discount structures can result in a net increase in advertising per dollar spent without a loss in media effectiveness.
   Media Efficiency - The media plan continually searches for the best media buy. CPM along with other measures should be used in order to select media as carefully as possible.
   Media Availability - If the media are not available or restrictions make it unavailable for the particular advertiser, then that media should not be included in the media plan.
   Competition - What the customer is used to in terms of media for the particular type of business can have a bearing on media choice.
   Nature of the Product - Where is the product in the life cycle? Is the product a member of a family of products or must it stand alone? The situation that the product is in should influence the media plan due to different levels of advertising need.
   Promotion Mix - A heavy emphasis on personal selling means that the media plan will utilize fewer ads than if a heavy emphasis is placed on advertising.

16-2   Although dependent upon the marketing objectives and marketing strategy of the firm, media objectives can and should be viewed as the heart of the media plan. The goal of such objectives is to translate marketing objectives and strategies into goals that media can accomplish by means of strategies and tactics. It is noted that the more precise and/or quantified the objectives are stated, the more effective they are as tools for use in the development of the media plan.

16-3   The national plan is a media strategy whose goal is the lowest possible CPM while reaching as much of the population as possible. The key-market plan is a media strategy whose goal is to reach as much of the population as possible in selected markets. The skim plan is a media strategy whose goal is to reach a carefully defined market. Which is better? The answer depends on the desired media objectives and strategies of the advertiser.

16-4   No - for a given amount of money, more frequency can only be obtained at the expense of reach. More dominance means less continuity as well as less coverage. The media strategy is a juggling act among the variables. The advertiser must determine what media strategy should be followed. To do so, decisions must be made about the relative importance to the advertiser of coverage, reach, frequency, continuity and dominance.

16-5   Continuity is a media strategy whose goal is a continuous program of advertising. It is much more than just running ads on a continuous basis. The actual advertisements over time should reenforce earlier ads. Slogans, trade characters, jingles, and logos are all widely used continuity vehicles. Continuity works on the same premise as repetition. It allows the advertisements over time to reenforce themselves for the benefit of the advertiser. As for dominance, it is defined as a media strategy whose goal is to give impact to the advertising program. The advertiser can dominate the advertising environment by having longer ads, bigger ads, color ads, bleed ads, ads in preferred positions, and anything else that will make the ads stand out from the crowd. Like the other elements of media strategy, dominance can normally be accomplished but it will be done at the expense of other strategy variables. As noted in the previous question, it becomes a situation where the advertiser must make hard strategy choices.

16-6   Tactics involving media scheduling are:
           Steady schedule - placement of the same size ad every day.
           Alternating-even schedule - placement of the same size ad every other
               day or at some other regular interval.
           Alternating-staggered schedule - placement of ads on a size rotation
               basis every other day or at some other regular interval. Provides
               a means for obtaining a certain level of dominance in the market
               place due to the occasional large ad.
           Pulse schedule - heavy ad placements are spaced at three- to four-week
               intervals. Also known as flighting. Greatest benefit is that
               it allows a limited advertising budget to go farther without a
               loss of dominance or continuity.
           Seasonal schedule - heavy ad placements are made during the appropriate
               buying season for the product.
           Step-up schedule - ad placements that begin with teaser ads and build
               to an advertising stage with a high level of dominance.
           Step-down schedule - ad placements that begin with a major advertising
               effort with a high level of dominance and then taper off.
       It should be noted that the choice of tactics depends upon the market conditions under which the product must be sold. Also, some media hamper certain tactic applications. Outdoor advertising, for example, must be bought by the month. It would, therefore, be impossible to use a three week flight plan with such media in the mix.

16-7   Pulsing does not appear to hurt effectiveness if done properly. So long as the time interval for no advertising does not exceed four weeks, the impact on the cumulative effect of advertising appears to be minimal. In fact, some say that the advertising wear-our rate (rate at which recall or learning declines over time) promotes pulsing since it diminishes the chances for overkill. Since pulsing does allow a limited advertising budget to go further with no harmful effects on effectiveness, pulsing is becoming a very popular media tactic for many advertisers.

16-8   Your student's opinion of media planning models will usually be influenced by his/her quantitative background as well as the level of computer understanding. In your discussion, stress that such models are tools of media planning, not plans in themselves that automatically provide an answer that should be followed by the advertiser. Visits with advertisers on this question should also be enlightening. For most businesses, it will be found that no media planning models are used. In fact, many firms will reveal to your students that no media planning at all is done for the firm. The exercise should be an interesting taste of real-world experience for your students.

16-9   The cumulative effect of advertising or advertising carryover is the length of time that an advertisement or a series of advertisements affects the ad recipient after the advertisements have been run. Studies indicate that advertising does appear to have this carryover effect. As noted by Alfred Kuehn, the effect of sales-price advertising is less than the impact of institutional advertising in terms of carryover. Why is carryover effect of interest to advertisers? Advertising on a continuing basis appears to give more clout to the advertising program. Each ad builds on each previous ad in such a way that the synergistic effect of the ad series results in more impact per ad for the advertising program. The media plan should consider this synergistic effect by scheduling ads on a regular basis throughout the media planning period.

16-10   One of the greatest benefits of media buying stems from the media schedules that are developed to show exactly what ads will be run where, and when. This approach encourages coordination while it aids in spotting problems such as gaps that are too long between ad flights and too limited coverage for particular selected markets. It would also be significant to point out to the advertiser friend that paying the rate card rate may be paying too much. It can be worthwhile to the advertiser to know that many media will sell below the printed rate if they feel impelled to do so. The smart advertiser will be aware of this fact and should strive to obtain the cheaper rate.

CHAPTER 17 - ADVERTISING RESEARCH AND
EVALUATION

17-1   By definition, marketing research is the systematic gathering, recording, and analyzing of data about problems relating to the marketing of goods and services. Advertising research, on the other hand, is the systematic gathering, recording, and analyzing of data dealing with the effectiveness of the advertising message and/or its delivery vehicle. The two types of research are copartners. Marketing research can be used to study the target market while advertising research can be used to determine if the message and the media are appropriate for the market.

17-2   The basic research procedure for almost any type of research consists of six steps:
            Problem Definition - Should be clearly stated. Be aware of the
                difference between the problem and a symptom of the problem.
            Secondary-Data Collection - Is the needed information already available?
            Primary-Data Collection - May be collected by observation, survey,
                or experimentation.
            Data Analysis - What information is obtained from the data?
            Data Presentation - Presentation of the findings in a clear and
                concise manner is important for acceptance.

      Followup - The findings, if appropriate, should be applied with
        an evaluation of the results being done at a later time.

17-3   The list of secondary sources for an advertiser of any type may include:
        Internal data - sales performance by product line, etc.
        Trade association data
        Trade publications
        Government data and publications
        Purchased information from Nielsen and others
In every instance, the original purpose for the data collection should be
determined. Information of this nature helps to determine the creditability
level of the data.

17-4   Primary-data collection procedures usually involve collecting data by means of
observation, survey, or experimentation from a sample of the target market
population. Although probability samples are more desirable, nonprobability
samples are more popular due to time and cost constraints. As for the first
research method, observation allows a study to work with no artificial stimulus.
This plus is also its greatest problem - observation must wait for something
to happen. The second approach, surveys, may be done by telephone (quick),
mail (convenient), or personal interview (in-depth information). The last
approach, experimentation, makes use of the test market/control market approach
or it may involve pure research into a problem that is difficult to define.
Advertisers can use these approaches to test copy, media, or some combination
of the two.

17-5   DAGMAR (Defining Advertising Goals for Measured Advertising Results) sets a
goal for a particular time frame which is then compared to results over time.
If the goal is met, the assumption is that the goal of the advertising program
was met. No attempt is made to prove that sales or whatever else was included
in the goal changed as a direct result of advertising. At its best, DAGMAR is
a rational planned approach to advertising evaluation. It, unfortunately, does
not solve the numerous problems associated with advertising evaluation when
that evaluation attempts to directly relate advertising with sales or some other
variable. DAGMAR is a planning tool. It is not a procedure that provides all
the answers for the advertiser in terms of advertising evaluation.

17-6   The choice between pretest and posttest depends on the needs of the advertiser.
The advantage of pretest rests with the fact that mistakes such as poor ads can
be caught early while its main disadvantage is that a pretest might not fully
represent a real market situation. The advantage and disadvantage discussed are
reversed for posttesting. Another problem with posttesting centers around the
dilemma of whether advertising alone caused the sale. Obviously, other elements
in the marketing mix could have an influence on sales and probably should do so.
The question of pretest vs posttest has no answer. Perhaps, the best answer is
to use both approaches to advertising evaluation.

17-7   The purpose of this exercise is to get students involved with a pretesting
procedure. It is recommended that the cartoon approach be the technique to be
used. It is less involved than other projective procedures as well as less
time consuming. The question as given should also reveal to your students that
different people view things in different ways. Hopefully, the target market
will view the ad in the desired manner. The projective pretest will help to
provide an answer as to how the target market does view the ad.

48

17-8   Laboratory techniques for use in pretesting include:
        Galvanic Skin Response (GSR) - Known as the sweaty palms test, GSR
            measures tension as shown by the level of perspiration in the
            hand vs the forearm.
        Voice-Pitch Analysis (VOPAN) - Measures the change in voice pitch
            as an indicator of emotional response.
        Brain-Pattern Analysis - Measures brain waves as an indicator of
            emotional response.
        Eye Tracking - Measures which part of an ad attracts the eye.
        Pupillary Analysis - Measures changes in the diameter of the pupil
            of the eye as an indicator of ad interest.
        Exposure Comprehension - Measures the length of exposure time that
            an ad requires for proper comprehension and perception.
    Although opinions will vary about the worth of such tests, students usually favor
    these tests because the results are measurable.

17-9   Recognition versus recall is not a question of which is better. It is a question
    of which type of information the advertiser wishes to have in terms of evaluation.
    Recognition studies measure if the ad was remembered by the reader of the
    publication and if that ad was read by the reader (ads are shown to the
    respondent). As for recall, the procedure asks the respondent to describe
    a particular ad without being shown the ad. Can the person recall what the
    ad looked like (advertising registration), what the sales message or selling
    points were (idea communication), and if the ad made the respondent want the
    product (favorable attitude)? Both methods have a place in posttesting. Each
    has a different purpose.

17-10   It is very difficult to measure the sales effectiveness of advertising. In some
    cases, it is impossible. In other cases, such as for direct mail, the inquiries
    that result from the mail piece can be correlated with sales. Customer diaries
    and test market vs control market procedures are also applicable to sales
    effectiveness studies. Depending on the assumptions to be made in the
    measurement model, the sales effectiveness of advertising can be studied. Of
    course, if the assumptions are incorrect, effectiveness measures become academic
    exercises with little or no use for the advertiser.

CHAPTER 18 - ADVERTISING AND THE MARKETING
PROGRAM

18-1   A marketing plan is a blueprint of all the marketing activities that are planned
    for a given period. It includes advertising, publicity, sales promotion, and
    personal selling as well as the products to be emphasized, price considerations,
    place variables, and personality (image) factors. A well-thought-out marketing
    plan can reap great rewards for a firm because all parts of the marketing
    effort are planned in light of all other parts of the plan. It makes good sense
    to develop a marketing plan because it promotes coordination within advertising,
    within the promotion mix, and within the marketing mix. As a planning tool, the
    development of a marketing plan is a smart business practice.

18-2   Coordination is a management term. It can also be a term that describes the
    process by which all parts of the advertising program work together, all parts
    of the promotion mix work together, and all parts of the marketing mix work
    together. Coordination belongs in advertising and marketing. Without it,
    the different parts of the advertising program could conflict with each other

so that the goal of sending the desired message by the best media at the appropriate time would not be fulfilled. Needless to say, the larger the firm and/or the larger the campaign, the greater the need for coordination. But any firm, regardless of size, should make the necessary effort to develop each marketing element in light of all other parts of the marketing program.

18-3   The campaign theme is an effective device for achieving coordination in advertising since it ties together the many different advertisements for a product. The theme for any particular campaign may take the form of a slogan, personality spokesperson, advertising format, or logo. By examining current campaigns, your students should begin to see the role that themes play in overall advertising strategy. A suggestion for the assignment is to direct your students to various issues of Time, Newsweek, Sports Illustrated, and similar magazines. Have them analyze the ads for the same products over a certain time span to see what efforts have been made to tie the various ads together.

18-4   Cooperative advertising may involve either an advertising program or an individual ad that is jointly sponsored by firms at the same level of a channel of distribution (horizontal) or by different members of a channel of distribution (vertical). As for the advantages and disadvantages of the latter, advantages include local rates (local/retail rates may be used instead of general rates), joint identity (a well-known product and a well-known store can help each other out), and channel encouragement (co-op plans tend to promote cooperation) while disadvantages include lack of control (is the money being spent wisely?), clerical problems (the handling of co-op claims can become an enormous task), legal problems (all firms must receive proportional assistance under Robinson-Patman), and channel resentment (neither party under many situations feels that the other is doing all it should to help sell the product. A feeling of distrust is also common which results in an adversary relationship instead of a cooperative one.).

18-5   Advertising can be sold as a buyer benefit to the trade market. When selling to the trade market, the advertiser can stress how the product/service/idea will be advertised to the ultimate consumer. The trade ads may name consumer magazines, television shows, etc., where the consumer ads will appear. Such information can also be aimed to the trade market by the firm's salespeople. What the advertiser is doing is telling the channel that a demand will be stimulated and that the channel should get ready by stocking the product. If correct, this information is a true buyer benefit for the channel. You might ask your students to take a look at various trade magazines (Progressive Grocer and Chain Store Age Supermarket are two good sources) to see examples of how manufacturers present consumer advertising as a buyer benefit.

18-6   Sales promotion includes all those activities, either nonrecurring or continuous, that supplement the advertising and personal selling effort of the firm. In checking with firms in your area, it will probably be noted by your students that most firms have no clear-cut concept about sales promotion. As for forms in use, coupons, contests, trading stamps, and premiums will be the most common for most firms. It will also probably be noted that most firms use this area of promotion on a sporadic basis. Like other types of promotion, many firms will not give evidence of any real planning in the area of sales promotion.

18-7   Do coupons work? The evidence indicates that coupons do have the potential to be an effective selling tool. One study cited in the book indicated that 48 percent of coupon users actively look for coupons. In addition, better than 7 out of 10 families with three or more persons with the homemaker in the

50

30- to 50-year-old age group use coupons regularly. In terms of redemption, it is noted that coupons in- or on-the-pack have higher levels of usage than any other method of distribution. If more information is desired, check current periodicals concerning the latest coupon data or contact the A. C. Nielsen Company for their latest findings. The address for A. C. Nielsen Company is Nielsen Plaza, Northbrook, Illinois 60062.

18-8   A skill contest is one in which the contestant is asked to do something that is then judged in some manner. In a chance contest, on the other hand, luck is the determining factor in deciding on who is the winner. In developing a contest, the advertiser must be aware of the FTC rules which require, among other things, that the numerical odds of winning each prize must be stated and that all prizes must be awarded as advertised. Care should also be taken to insure that the contest does not run into trouble with lottery statutes. As a general rule, it is better not to require the customer to buy the product in order to take part, even if it is a skill contest. Of course, most will buy the product, service, etc. anyway, since it will be easier than writing the name of the product in block letters on a 3 x 5 card or some other alternative to buying the product as is required in many contests.

18-9   A premium is an item that is given or sold to a customer after the customer has met his/her obligation. Premiums may be distributed with the product (toy in cereal), in the store (try the product out and get a free coke), or by the manufacturer (send in a proof-of-purchase seal and get a free ballpoint pen). They may also be sold at cost (self-liquidator) or even at a profit but all will require proof of purchase or some other type of obligation. Third, premiums may be one-time promotions or continuous (select a new piece of cookware each week with a minimum purchase of $10). Continuous promotions are designed to solicit repeat traffic over the life of the promotion.

18-10   Sampling - A form of sales promotion that provides the customer with a portion of the actual product at little or no cost to the customer. A sample gives people the chance to try the product. More effective than a coupon since it actually places the product in the customer's hands.
Trading Stamps - A form of sales promotion that provides the customer with fractional certificates that are redeemable for merchandise and/or cash. The purpose of stamps is to build repeat business by those who have the stamp habit. The rural, older market is the more favorable market for using stamps.
Price Deals - A form of sales promotion which involves any planned method of price reduction. Common forms include cash rebates (customer receives money from the manufacturer after a product purchase), cents-off promotions (a 12 percent reduction may be needed to generate additional customer interest), and combination offers (cost of the two items bought together is less than each bought separately).
Demonstrations - A form of sales promotion which shows the customer the product in use. "Seeing is believing" does appear to sell many products.
Exhibits - A form of sales promotion that may be self-supporting or used in conjunction with personal selling; its purpose is to sell the product by attracting people to the exhibit site. Although gaining in popularity in the consumer market, the mainstay of exhibit use continues to be the business trade show.

CHAPTER 19 - ADVERTISING APPLICATIONS

19-1   The retail ad should stress the store as well as the product. Many small stores cannot compete with larger stores in terms of price or name-brand products. What they can compete with is the store itself. How many supermarkets sell Coca-Cola and Tide? Probably every one of them. To advertise Coca-Cola may be a traffic-builder if the price is reduced but an ad for Coca-Cola will do nothing to build customer identity with the store. The smart retailer sells his/her store. The ads that are collected will in most cases stress products which may not be desirable from a retail advertising standpoint. Most retail ads are not very effective. Basically, they do not sell benefits, have little creativity, and do not attract the attention of the target market or anyone else.

19-2   Retail advertising sells to the ultimate consumer whereas business advertising sells to the retailer as well as other business types. The objective of much business advertising is to pave the way for the forthcoming sales call on the business firm while the objective of the retail ad is to generate consumer traffic for the store. Since the customers are different, the reasons for purchase (buyer benefits) will be different. The retailer ad for Hanes will stress that "gentlemen prefer Hanes" while the business ad may stress what consumer advertising is being used to sell the product, which price deals may be used, what new shades and styles of hose will be coming soon, and other types of information which is of interest to the business customer who expects to make money by selling Hanes hosiery to the consumer market.

19-3   For business advertising, a common media mix might consist of business magazines and direct mail whereas a retail mix might utilize newspapers, radio, television, and outdoor, along with direct mail. Of course, there is actually no typical media mix since the needs of firms vary so greatly. The differences that do exist between retail advertising and business advertising are a function of the scope of advertising and the role it plays in the selling of the product. Personal selling is assigned most of the promotional task in the business market whereas advertising is given a greater role to play in selling to the consumer. Customer differences is what makes retail advertising and business advertising two distinct entities.

19-4   Service advertising is advertising that sells an intangible that requires no transfer of ownership to complete the sale. Services are sold and then produced which is the opposite of product advertising where the product is normally produced and then sold. Services are usually promoted in such a way as to project an image of dependability, competence, and the ability to meet the needs of the customer. Testimonials can be a very effective tool. Any effort that attempts to make the service appear tangible should increase interest and sales. A statement to the effect that the business has been around for a long time will also prove to be a plus for the service ad.

19-5   The eight different types of demand for nonprofit services are:
          Negative demand - people are willing to pay to avoid it.
                (draft registration ads promote the idea that registration
                is a duty, not an obligation)
          No demand - people are indifferent.
                ("Teeth brushing is smart" - says the public service ad
                aimed at children)
          Latent demand - people have a strong need for the product
                (safe cars are important)

Faltering demand - people demand less of the product
(more working parents means less involvement/interest in
family, religious, and civic activities. Ads try to
counter the problem by pointing it out.)
Irregular demand - demand is predictable but volatile.
(many national parks have peak demand periods followed by
low utilization. Ads attempt to get people to use the parks
during the off season.)
Full demand - demand has reached the limit
(Ads for certain national parks attempt to get people to have
short stays and perhaps even not plan to come as often.)
Overfull demand - demand has exceeded all reasonable limits. Will
actually attempt to demarket the product.
(the goal would be to switch people to other public parks,
not just call for short visits.)
Unwholesome demand - candy ads for children are unwholesome. If
this judgment decision is made, then ads that sell children
on the idea that candy is bad will be considered nonprofit
advertising.

19-6   The Ad Council is an organization that is <u>not</u> funded by the federal government
nor does it control all forms of public service advertising. The Council is the
coordinating body for most national donated nonprofit advertising campaigns. It
consists of 85 board members who represent all segments of the advertising industry.
Once approved by the Board, the nonprofit campaign is assigned to a volunteer
agency and a volunteer coordinator from industry is selected. The ads are then
developed and the media donate time and space to bring the message to the public.

19-7   The purpose of political advertising is to present a cause, a candidate, or both
in a favorable way so that the decision maker will be influenced to act in
the desired manner. Such advertising does not appear to be a waste of funds.
In one study, over half of the respondents indicated that their awareness of a
political issue had come through some form of advertising. In more than one
election, the candidate that becomes a household word due to repetitive
advertising has been victorious. Did advertising make the difference? So long
as people think so, political advertising will continue to be a part of the
political system. As noted in the question, have your students research this
question in the current literature. There should be pertinent articles on the
topic in 1980 sources as a presidential election always creates interest in
this topic.

19-8   Institutional advertising, which is sometimes called corporate advertising,
consists of public relations advertising whose primary goal is to sell the
organization to its many publics. Advocacy advertising, on the other hand,
attempts to sell an idea that is favorable to the company or organization.
With advocacy advertising, care should be taken not to oversell. Some may say
that "where there is smoke, there is fire." Too much advocacy can backfire on
a company. A high level of credibility is crucial for a successful advocacy
advertisement. As for current examples, issues such as pollution, environment,
good citizenship, and so on, may be cited by your students. As skeptical
students, most reactions to such ads will usually be negative or neutral. As
advertising students, please emphasize to them that "typical" consumers may not
be so negative toward such ads.

19-9   A press kit is a collection of facts and figures, photographs, and other information that will make the task of telling the advertiser's desired story an easy one for the media. The best reason for developing such a kit is that it enhances the publicity efforts of the company and, thereby, increases the probability that the desired story will be presented to the public by means of the media.

19-10   In order to answer this question, the student can provide feedback as to what is in the book under each of the five topic areas or a better idea is to go to The Wall Street Journal, other business papers, various international periodicals, and even talk with students from various countries that may be on campus and present an updated look at the ever changing world of international advertising. If the class is large and resources are plentiful, you could assign each student or student team to a particular group of countries and have each one report the findings to the class. The end result will be a composite picture of how different advertising really is in the different countries of the world.

CHAPTER 20 - ADVERTISING TRENDS

20-1   Each year, numerous journals and other sources recap the year and then predict what the future holds for advertising. The trends as given in the chapter can be updated by using these sources and by talking to people in the advertising industry concerning their ideas on the future. To predict the future is never easy but students usually enjoy the effort. As an interesting long term project, have your students summarize their future predictions on 3 x 5 cards and then file them away for several years or even ten years if space permits. Their predictions will make interesting reading for your advertising class ten years from now. The only thing that is certain about predicting the future of advertising is that change will take place.

20-2   Obviously, a career in advertising may not even involve writing ads, much less sitting behind a desk. To assist you in leading the discussion on this question, it is recommended that you obtain the two publications that are cited in note 3 for the chapter. They will be extremely helpful in career counseling as well as in making this question serve as a means of bringing to light all the various career choices in advertising.

SECTION III

SUGGESTED SOLUTIONS TO
CASES/EXPERIENTIAL LEARNING EXERCISES

The cases/experiential learning exercises as given in the text do not have one particular solution. Depending on the student's background, the resources available, and the time allotted to the exercise, the solutions given by your students can vary widely in terms of depth of topic coverage. It should be noted that the exercises call for the student to assume a role that is not that of an advertising student. Instead, the student is asked to put on the hat of a person who must make advertising decisions and in some cases to create ads as well. Either individually or in groups, your students will experience learning by doing by working with one or more of these exercises. Based on my own classroom experience, I strongly recommend that you give your students some hands-on advertising exposure by using the cases/experiential learning exercises provided in the text.

#1
AMERICAN GENERAL PRODUCTS CORPORATION

It is obvious that the makers of <u>Wunderpil</u> have a potential legal problem. In addressing this problem, the student should elaborate on the NAD-NARB procedure as outlined in Figure 3-4 in the book. Also, a check of various issues of <u>Advertising Age</u> will reveal the actions taken by NAD-NARB. The student might also review the various FTC actions taken in the past as found in <u>Federal Trade Commission Decisions</u>, a federal publication. This should give some idea of potential FTC action in this case. It is noted that due to the nature of the case, it is quite possible that the FTC might order the firm to run a counter ad campaign. Be sure that your students search out the current legal status of this FTC technique. In the <u>Listerine</u> case, the advertiser lost the case but many legal minds do not feel that the Supreme Court ruling gave a blanket endorsement to the counter ad concept. A check of <u>The Wall Street Journal</u> and <u>Advertising Age</u> as well as various advertising and legal journals should provide insight into this legal question in terms of its current status. In developing the position paper, it is possible that the firm's ads may also be reviewed by the ANA in cooperation with AAAA. Although no public response will result from this inquiry, this review board may also request that the firm cease any advertising that may be thought to be misleading. In addressing the various options that may be available to the makers of <u>Wunderpil</u>, the position paper should stress that NAD-NARB and other procedures will normally permit the firm to change its advertising approach or to cease the advertising campaign without future penalty if the campaign has been used for only a short period of time. Only if the firm fails to take action will a stronger remedy be called for by the various public and private organizations.

#2
AMERICAN ACADEMY OF ADVERTISING SEMINAR

This experiential learning exercise will get your students involved in the process of understanding how the four elements of the advertising industry work together as well as the strong points and weak points of each. The basic list of strong and weak points for each industry segment can be developed from the material found in Chapter 4. The discussion generated by the exercise should serve to illustrate that the strong points of one industry segment counter the weak points of a different industry segment. Where possible, you might request that your students solicit the advice of advertising practitioners from their particular industry segment to aid them in their preparation for the "seminar." Although the list of strong points and weak points can be quite lengthy and varied for each industry segment, selected items for each segment list are as follows:

Advertising Department

Strong Points	Weak Points
May obtain local rates as opposed to commission rates.	May not be objective in terms of what is best for advertising.
Company has better control over advertising personnel.	May lack knowledge due to working on a few accounts (synergistic experience).
More time is available to learn about company products.	Usually limited in terms of production capability.
Offers possibility of last minute flexibility.	May be expensive due to cost of carrying company overhead.
Easy to coordinate advertising effort with rest of marketing effort.	May be assigned other duties for company without adequate personnel, thereby hurting advertising effort.

Advertising Agency

Strong Points

Due to semi-independent nature, agency may be more objective.

Synergistic experience - knowledge gained from other clients can be helpful.

Full-service agency may permit centralization of advertising effort.

A strong pool of advertising personnel with specialized talents.

May be less expensive in long run due to better quality of advertising product.

Weak Points

May not be able to learn the client well due to number.

If client is small, agency may not devote adequate effort.

Agency commissions/fees/charges can be expensive.

Sometimes difficult to coordinate advertising with rest of marketing effort.

Agency may not have expertise in area served by client.

Special Service Groups

Strong Points

Specialization promotes quality of product.

May be able to perform that special job better due to scale of operation.

Job may be done cheaper due to specialization.

Permits advertising departments and agencies to concentrate on most needed services by providing them the rarely needed ones.

Allows a one-person advertising department or agency to offer a full-range of services to a client.

Weak Points

Coordination of various efforts can be difficult.

Difficult to obtain complete understanding of marketing program of client.

Advertising changes and corrections are difficult with many firms involved.

No centralization of authority, responsibility, and accountability for advertising effort.

Many special service firms only available in major advertising centers.

Media

Strong Points

Convenient to have ads created and run by media.

Out-of-pocket costs for ad development may be minimal.

Allows small firm to develop ads by using the production facilities of the media.

Flexibility in terms of last minute changes is usually available.

Provides advice on local market conditions.

Weak Points

Media representative may have limited advertising knowledge.

Lack of objectivity when recommending media mix.

Media representative's pay method related to ad sales, not ad quality.

With different media involved, coordination is difficult.

May attempt to play one advertiser against another in order to promote ad revenue.

#3
JOE'S FINE FOODS

From the information provided, it would appear that the restaurant needs to be positioned in some manner in the market. It is possible that the name of the restaurant should be changed and even the menu. The astute student will note from the case that no mention is made of the target market. Before Joe should do anything, the target market must be defined in as great a detail as possible. After this is done, the marketing mix should be addressed (Product, Price, Place, Promotion, and Personality). Hard decisions should be made which will help lay the foundation for the USP and copy platform. In addition, market analysis and product analysis are called for along with decisions pertaining to the choice of advertising strategies and advertising objectives. With the proper foundation now in place, the unique selling proposition and copy platform for the restaurant can be developed with confidence. As for what the USP and copy platform should be for the restaurant, the answer depends on what the students have done and/or assumed up to this point in the advertising process. In all cases, however, emphasis should be placed on uniqueness in terms of USP. The failure to offer the customer something to set the restaurant apart from the competition should cause the restaurant to continue its decline, which is not in the best interest of Joe or the advertising consultant.

#4
MICHELE'S

With a high-income market, the first task for your students is to determine what media in your area reach that market. The second task is to determine if any of the possible media lack the appropriate prestige image that is needed by a store selling cruise clothes to upper-income customers. Of the media listed, outdoor, transit, and many forms of specialty advertising may be eliminated in this second step. The next step in the process is to develop a media strategy that provides the desired levels of dominance, continuity, coverage, reach, and frequency. Considering the size of the appropriation, television and magazines may have to be eliminated from consideration. Radio may also be eliminated if no station in the market area attempts to market itself to the defined target market. With its limited budget, Michele's should probably rely on newspaper and direct media for the major portion of the advertising thrust. As for directory advertising, the Yellow Pages is not viable although the firm will have a listing as a result of having a business phone. The only possible directory ad may be one in a social directory of some type such as a directory of members as published by a Country Club. Even here, the ad will be placed more for image than for direct cause-effect advertising purposes. As your students develop the list of media and why they did or did not choose them, the pros and cons given should be a mixture of the advantages and disadvantages of the media as provided in Appendix B and the unique pluses and minuses of your local media. The latter ideas should be of interest to your local media. As for the actual ads, this exercise will provide your students with the opportunity to try their hand at ad creation. It is suggested that you not expand on the information given in the book concerning what type of store Michele's is or what you would do. The more input you give before the assignment is due, the more you will restrict your students' imaginations and their creativity.

58

#5
SONGS UNLIMITED

Since the firm chooses to be a direct marketer, your students should develop one
or more mail pieces which could be used to sell the "golden oldies." Equally important
as the mail pieces is who will receive the mail pieces. If the SRDS direct mail books
are available to your students, allow them to choose where they would send the
advertisements. In most situations, a rented list will be more preferable than a
compiled list. Also, a list of people who have bought records by mail will be desirable.
An internal list of customers who have bought other records from Songs Unlimited
would also be a good potential list of names. As for what the mail piece should look
like, creativity will determine the answer but certain elements which would usually be
included are a letter using two-color text, a second letter, a bedsheet or another type
of color illustration, an action order form and an envelope for use in returning the
order form. Although cost is said not to be a factor, students who create expensive
mail pieces should be reminded that management wanted practical solutions costing
realistic dollars. One other point in the case that your students may react to is the
television ad that calls for action in such a way that its impact is lost on the
regular TV viewer. You might solicit ideas from the class on whether the "offer ends
at midnight" technique is a problem. A check of broadcast stations in your area may
yield information concerning how these ads generate business over time. You might
also ask your class to come up with another action close for the ad. One possibility
could be, "Act now, this offer may be withdrawn at any time!" As for what the promotion
mix for the firm should be, the choice is up to the management of Songs Unlimited. The
direct mail pieces, as developed, combined with the ideas on how to improve the television
advertisements should give the firm the kind of assistance that should be of help to
them in putting together a better direct marketing package.

#6
STANTEX PETROLEUM COMPANY

This case is particularly applicable if your students are either majoring in or
have an interest in public relations. As the exercise emphasizes, Stantex does not
wish to "overkill" the public by coming on too strong. As is true with other forms
of advertising, a public relations/service campaign needs to begin with a definition
of the target market, a market analysis, a product analysis, a determination of
advertising objectives and a determination of USP. Once it is determined what ideas
need to be presented, the actual ads and the media choices can be decided. In order
to determine how the $5 million might be allocated, national rates as provided by SRDS
and published reports in Advertising Age and similar sources for network television,
etc., will tell the student how much various media schedules will cost the advertiser.
It should be interesting to see if your students attempt to apply the task method of
budget appropriation or if they will automatically plan to spend the entire $5 million
as allocated. It is predicted that most will follow the latter course of action. Also,
as your students put together the media plan, note to see if they follow any recognized
form of scheduling. Long intervals of time with no advertising are not desirable
even for advertising of a public service nature. Finally, a look at the actual ads will
really reflect in some cases how your students view petroleum companies. Some ads will
reflect directly the company's relationship to oil while others will go far afield in
order to present the company in a favorable light. Also, remember that this campaign
is national in scope. Depending on the approach taken, some ads may be regional in
orientation and, therefore, placed in the appropriate regional media or in regional
editions of national media while others will apply to the national market. Upon
completion of this exercise, your students will probably never again view lightly the

task of putting together a public relations advertising campaign. In many ways, a public service program is more difficult to develop than is one for a tangible product.

#7
HOTDOGS BY HARRY

The case illustrates the problem of following what the media suggests should be done. Under this media arrangement, coordination is almost impossible. Little planning is undertaken. The quality of the ads will also probably be low. Needless to say, for these and other reasons, your students should take issue with the passive role for the advertising manager that is suggested by Harry Smith. But wait, the case exercise stated that the procedure worked pretty well in the past. With the cost of media being what it is, not to mention the possibility that a better advertising effort could result if the advertiser took a more active role, the luxury of having a procedure work pretty well is not good enough. But suppose Harry Smith did change his mind after he was told the above deficiencies for his current procedure, what then? First, the student (advertising manager) should be concerned with market analysis and product analysis. Advertising strategies and objectives would follow next with the end result being a copy platform for Hotdogs by Harry. Using the copy platform, the ads would be produced for placement in the appropriate media for the target market. Procedures relating to budgeting, media planning, research, and the fitting of advertising into the overall marketing program should also be implemented. In other words, everything discussed in the book from Chapter 5 to Chapter 18 or the 3 M's of advertising (Message, Media, Management) should be touched on as your students outline what procedures should be implemented by the advertising manager for Hotdogs by Harry. This case is a good assignment for the last few days of the session, or can be used as a final exam question since it asks students to summarize each of the elements of the course and equally important, to show that they understand that the 3 M's work together although they were presented separately for purposes of discussion.

#8
COLLINS, INC.

Collins, Inc. provides the student with an opportunity to be creative on behalf of the client. This assignment, which can be done on an individual basis or in teams, allows the student to gain "hands-on" advertising experience. As for the different parts of the assignment, care should be taken not to make the product name descriptive or deceptive. A name like "B.O." or "Smell" would be undesirable. Names that might be used successfully are "Life," "Success," "Mr. C," and "Friend In Need." You might have fun with this last name. By assigning "Friend In Need," or some similar name, you will force your students to be creative. You and they will probably be surprised at how creative students can be under pressure. As for the package, innovation is important. How will it stand out on the shelf? If you wish, direct your students to make a 3-dimensional mock-up of the package. Then, when the assignment is due, surprise your students by bringing to class packages of existing products off the shelves of a drug store. (These can usually be borrowed for such purposes.) Now, each student can see how his/her package compares with the competition. When ads are studied, much depends on the copy platform. Each platform should be developed using the target market as defined by that student or group. As for what else might be done, the area of sales promotion was mentioned. Coupons and contests are two definite possibilities to go along with the proposed sampling plan and premium. In advertising, specialty advertising and direct mail media should be given serious considerations along with other media when students assumptions make them appropriate. Appropriate avenues for publicity should also be pursued. It is noted that both consumer- and trade-related promotional efforts are a must. Many of your students will forget the push element and will, instead, concentrate on media pull (consumer ads). Like most exercises, Collins, Inc., has no one set solution. It should be interesting to see how different people approach the exercise. It is recommended that you let your students see what others did and even, perhaps, let them pick the one they like best from all those submitted. A certain level of competitive rivalry should promote interest in the assignment.

#9
KICKLIGHTER ENTERPRISES

Does a person want to use a product that will "kick the dirt out of your rug?" The slogan has a problem. It implies that it might be rough on a fine or delicate carpet. Also, the trade character leaves something to be desired. Does a mule imply quality, cleaniness, or any other positive qualities? The only identity connection most will make would be with 20 MULE TEAM (borax). This strong cleaner would be hard on fine carpets. As most people perceive the situation, neither slogan or trade character is considered a plus for the product. As for the name, it is possible that the firm could be sold on using a modified family branding procedure that would allow Kicklighter to be possessive of the brand - Kicklighter's _____ Rug Shampoo. This approach would work to lessen the impact of the negative side of the connotation of kick while still providing identity with the parent firm. Kicklighter's Carpet-Nu Rug Shampoo is just one of many examples that could be used by your students. As for the actual ad campaign, ads in both consumer and trade media should be developed. By using Standard Rate and Data Service books and other sources, a market area that is centered around Oklahoma should be established that will allow for appropriate reach, frequency, continuity, and dominance within the given $100,000 limitation. For trade media, Progressive Grocer, Chain Store Age Executive, American Druggist, and similar sources should be considered. As for consumer media, magazines with regional coverage, newspaper co-op, direct mail sampling, and point-of-purchase advertising should be considered. Your students should be expected to develop a detailed budget, media plan, and the actual ads to be run when using the plan. If radio ads are used, encourage your students to actually tape the ads. Having such ads makes the product come to life. Once again, you can make the assignment on an individual or team basis. Also, the amount of time given to the assignment should be reflected in the degree of effort and the complexity of work that should be expected of your students. If your students learn little else from this exercise, it will get the point across to them that $100,000 will not buy as much advertising as most students think it will buy. It can be an enlightening experience.

#10
ADVERTISING PROJECT

In the more than ten years that I have taught advertising, nothing has been more effective or created more interest than having students work with experiential learning exercise #10 as given in the book. The first day of the session, a product, appropriation, and time frame are given to the class. For example, a recent class advertised a solar music box that was sold in five southern states with a total appropriation of $50,000. Another class was assigned a pen with a light in the end for writing in the dark. That product also was marketed to five states with funding in the $50,000 range. Both of these campaigns were set up for one year. Other assignments that I have given include:

Maternity Shop (also sells to fat women)
Gift Shop
Children's Clothing Store
Sandwich Shop
Floral & Gift Shop

In each situation, each team (agency), must come up with the name of the store or product, select an appropriate target market after performing market analysis and then allocate the budget, develop the media plan, and create the actual ads. In the retailing examples, all budgets were set low - $10,000-$15,000 - and were for a 12 month period. In each instance, the store was said to be located at a particular site in the same town as the college. Another possibility for an assignment, as mentioned earlier in Section I of the Instructor's Manual, is to sell your town to the surrounding towns as a retail shopping center. In some cases, your local merchants association or Chamber of Commerce may have an interest in the project and may even use the results. Still another idea is to develop a campaign to sell your college or university. Assume that a rich person died and left $25,000 to promote the institution with paid media. This assumption removes the problems associated with public relations/ publicity and how to pay for ads at a state institution or other similar obstacles. An additional idea is to have your class work on a real project for a client. In many schools, Small Business Institute cases may involve an appropriate advertising situation. It could also be that a firm wants to get ideas by having your students develop speculative campaigns for their use. Depending on the policies of your institution, money to cover the cost of campaign development and even more for other uses may be raised through donations in return for services rendered by you and your students. As the course develops, your students will work on the project with a deadline near the end of the session for ad presentations. Unless the class is small, it is better to schedule these presentations in the late afternoon or evening so that all presentations can be given at the same time. Where available, an executive conference room or other similar facility that will hold the class plus visitors can be used for added effect. Since the presentation of a speculative campaign is very important in the real world of advertising, it should also be true in your advertising class. Visuals are very important. A business-like manner is vital as are time constraints. No presentation should be permitted to exceed its time limit. In addition to the presentation, an advertising campaign book should be prepared that includes all the elements of a well-planned advertising campaign. Appearance as well as content should be stressed. Upon completion of the presentations, ask your students to pick the one presentation they liked best, excluding their own. This can give you guidance and will usually drive home the idea that a good presentation is obvious since in almost all cases, one particular presentation will get a majority of the votes. If time permits, an evaluation session is helpful with each team (agency) sitting before the rest of the class and the instructor for a question/answer session. If your own knowledge of advertising makes you feel uncomfortable about this approach, you can, instead, provide a written critique of the project to each team after comparing what was done with the fundamental concepts as presented in the text. As was noted in Section I of the Instructor's Manual, you may have a campaign course where a project is conducted. If you do not have such a course, the campaign can be done in the introductory course. The exercise has proven to be very worthwhile. Not only do students learn advertising by doing but they also continue to use the campaign material as part of their job portfolio. The project is time-consuming. It is difficult. But when students are asked what experiences in college have contributed most to learning, many cite the advertising project. Give serious thought to making the advertising project an integral part of your advertising course. It will make it a better course.

EXAM QUESTIONS
CHAPTERS 1-20

Twelve hundred exam questions are provided for your use. Questions vary in terms of difficulty so as to allow you to develop an exam to meet your particular needs. The questions are divided by Chapter with the appropriate answer indicated to the left of each true-false and multiple choice question and in the space provided for each completion question. It is recommended that you use a mixture of test question forms on your exam. One or more of the discussion questions which are found at the end of each chapter may also be used.

CHAPTER 1 - ADVERTISING: AN OVERVIEW

True or False

T 1-1. Good advertising should inform and persuade the selected market.

F 1-2. The terms "sales promotion" and "advertising" can be used interchangeably.

T 1-3. Public service messages are included in advertising when you replace the term "paid" with "controlled" in the definition of advertising.

F 1-4. Since an advertisement is intended for a large mass of people, it seldom caters to a particular group or market.

T 1-5. Symbols were often used in early advertising because many people were illiterate.

F 1-6. "Word-of-mouth advertising" is easily controlled by a business. Because of this, it is one of the most effective forms of advertising.

F 1-7. Advertising as we know it today started in England in 1502.

T 1-8. The first "broadcast" advertisement was the town crier.

T 1-9. William Caxton is credited with using the first printed ad around 1480 to promote a book of ecclesiastical rules.

T 1-10. Some of the early town criers in France gave out wine samples on behalf of sponsoring taverns.

F 1-11. The "Mark of Excellence by GM" was one of the first trademarks used in the United States.

T 1-12. The printing of the Bible in 1450 by Gutenberg opened the way for printed advertising.

T 1-13. Some of the earliest documented advertising dates back to Babylonian times.

F 1-14. In 1741, Benjamin Franklin put out one of the first magazines in America but his American Magazine failed after 6 months.

F 1-15. The early advertising agents or space brokers provided the business firm with newspaper and magazine advertisements for a price.

F 1-16. Radio broadcast advertising got its start in 1895 in Pittsburgh, Pennsylvania.

T 1-17. Television as an advertising vehicle began in 1939 but its development was slowed by WWII.

F 1-18. Advertisers did not readily accept television as a medium because most of the early T.V. sets were located in small towns.

64

F   1-19.   Despite the advent of television, radio maintained its original status as
             a national medium until the late 1970's.

T   1-20.   Nearly $44 billion was spent on advertising in the United States in 1978.

F   1-21.   Television ranks first among media in terms of the level of current annual
             advertising expenditures in the United States.

F   1-22.   Product advertising seldom generates enough demand to cover its high
             advertising costs.

T   1-23.   Consumers are generally willing to pay more money for a well-known
             product/brand.

T   1-24.   The value of a product or store can be promoted or destroyed by the way it
             is advertised.

T   1-25.   Procter and Gamble is the U.S.'s biggest overall user of advertising in terms
             of dollars spent.

T   1-26.   Ad expenditures in the United States have been increasing in nearly every
             media form for the last several years.

T   1-27.   Newspaper advertising accounts for over one-fourth of all advertising
             dollars spent in the United States in a given year.

T   1-28.   Today, local radio ads are more common than network radio ads.

F   1-29.   A business should not expect advertising to have an impact on sales.

F   1-30.   In the years to come, we can expect little in terms of additional
             developments in the history of advertising.

Multiple Choice

A   1-31.   A definition of advertising includes all of the following except:
             A.   Personal presentation.
             B.   Promotion of a good, service, or idea
             C.   Known sponsor
             D.   Paid-for form
             E.   None of the above

E   1-32.   Advertising is often designed for a particular market segment. Of the
             following, which is not an example of a select market:
             A.   Pregnant women in New York
             B.   Migrant workers in California
             C.   College students
             D.   Brunettes in Idaho
             E.   None of the above

C   1-33. Early advertising took on which of the following forms?

       I. Shop signs   IV. Verbal announcements
      II. Guild marks   V. Handbills
     III. Radio broadcasts   VI. Word of mouth

      A. I, II, III, V
      B. I, IV, V
      C. I, II, IV, V
      D. I, II, III, V
      E. All of the above

E   1-34. Among the significant factors making the United States ready for advertising growth were:
      A. Rural free delivery
      B. Mass production
      C. Educated population
      D. Both A and B
      E. All of the above

D   1-35. The first edition of The Boston Newsletter, the first newspaper in the United States, was printed in the year:
      A. 1398
      B. 1492
      C. 1625
      D. 1704
      E. 1895

D   1-36. Subjects of early print advertising in The Boston Newsletter were all of the following except:
      A. Lost articles
      B. Real estate
      C. Slave sales
      D. Ship sales
      E. Runaway apprentices

B   1-37. Early advertising agents provided which of the following services:
      A. Assisted in ad set-up
      B. Bought and sold newspapers space
      C. Designed ads
      D. Wrote ad copy
      E. All of the above

C   1-38. All of the following are main functions of advertising except:
      A. To sell a good, service, or idea
      B. To aid in the customer's search process
      C. To create known brands that consumers will pay more for
      D. To persuade consumers to buy
      E. None or all of the above

66

C   1-39. Which of the following are examples of a service advertiser?
            I.   March of Dimes   IV. Savings & Loan
            II. Sears, Roebuck & Co.   V. Plumber
            III. Lawyer   VI. Restaurant

            A.   I, III, IV, V
            B.   II, III, IV, VI
            C.   III, IV, V, VI
            D.   I, II, IV, VI
            E.   All of the above

E   1-40. All of the following are advertising media except:
            A.   Business papers
            B.   Radio
            C.   Farm magazine
            D.   Billboards
            E.   All are examples of advertising media

E   1-41. Television advertising was readily accepted by advertisers because:
            A.   There were few T.V. stations
            B.   Results were traced quickly
            C.   T.V. ads were inexpensive to make
            D.   The growth of T.V. was in the metropolitan areas
            E.   A, B, and D are correct

E   1-42. Advertising promotes competition by:
            A.   Stabilizing the market share
            B.   Warding off new rivals
            C.   Creating brand loyalty
            D.   All of the above
            E.   None of the above

E   1-43. Prior to 1600, which of the following media were not used to advertise a
            product:
            A.   Newspaper
            B.   Handbills
            C.   Trademarks
            D.   Signs
            E.   All were used prior to 1600

E   1-44. It is a known fact that:
            A.   Advertising creates demand
            B.   Advertising promotes competition
            C.   Advertising adds value
            D.   Advertising makes products less expensive
            E.   None of the above are correct

D   1-49. The following is not an example of a commonly advertised good:
            A.   Processed T.V. dinner
            B.   Hamburger Helper
            C.   Vacuum cleaner
            D.   Airline travel
            E.   Gasoline

B 1-50. If advertising makes people aware of a product, they will generally prefer it over a product they have not heard of. This is an example of advertising:
A. Creating demand
B. Adding value
C. Promoting competition
D. All of the above
E. None of the above

Completion

1-51. Economist Philip Nelson believes that advertising increases consumer information about substitutes and that this reduces (_monopoly power_).

1-52. A sign or mark used as a form of brand differentiation is called a/an (_trademark_).

1-53. Developments in American advertising were significantly aided by the Industrial Revolution, the (_transportation system_), and the (_education_) (_system_).

1-54. Another name for free "advertising" that depends on what people tell others about a business is (_"word of mouth advertising"_).

1-55. Dating back to 1141 A.D., the (_town crier_) was the first "broadcast advertisement."

1-56. Printed advertising came into being shortly after the printing of the Bible by (_Gutenberg_) in 1450.

1-57. A/an (_space broker_) is an agent who promotes advertising by purchasing newspaper and magazine space and then selling it to business firms at a higher rate.

1-58. In terms of dollar level spent on advertising in the United States, (_newspapers_) are the most preferred media, with (_television_) holding second place.

1-59. In 1978, the total U.S. advertising expenditure was (_$43.8 billion_) as compared to the 1960 expenditure of $11.9 billion.

1-60. The main functions of advertising are to (_inform_) and to (_persuade_) the selected market.

CHAPTER 2 - ADVERTISING: ITS RELATIONSHIP TO MARKETING

True or False

F 2-1. Advertising messages should be advertiser-oriented.

F 2-2. The target market for Gerber's baby food in Dallas, Texas includes the population of Dallas.

68

T   2-3.   Advertising has played a major role in creating a "new market" for products that have traditionally been single-sex-oriented.

F   2-4.   Advertising is the most important element in the marketing mix.

T   2-5.   The consumer market is concerned with the ultimate consumption of the product while a business firm deals primarily with the development of products for resale.

F   2-6.   The marketing concept does not concern itself with profit.

F   2-7.   The industrial and institutional business markets are distinguishable in that the industrial market emphasizes service along with the physical product, while the institutional market emphasizes only the product.

T   2-8.   Derived demand is a factor in determining the product needs of an industrial market.

F   2-9.   An advertiser should periodically change or expand a product's target market.

F   2-10.   Retailers seeking information on how and where a particular finished product is being marketed, would look for such information in industrial ads.

T   2-11.   The trade market consists primarily of those firms who sell to the ultimate consumer.

T   2-12.   In the industrial market, products are purchased by industries from other industries in order to complete items to be sold to its various markets.

T   2-13.   There are business markets in which an advertised product is given away free of charge to the person/firm that is the primary target of the advertising campaign.

F   2-14.   Since the farm market is conservative, it prefers professional advertisements over testimonial ads.

T   2-15.   A good marketing mix coordinates the promotion, price, place, personality, and product plans and actions of the firm.

F   2-16.   Advertising is part of the promotion mix but not an element in the marketing mix.

F   2-17.   An automobile is one example of a staple good as it is dependent on place availability for purchase.

T   2-18.   Since chewing gum and Life Savers are frequently impulse purchases, they should be advertised at the point of sale.

F   2-19.   Price is the key element in advertisements for emergency goods.

F   2-20.   Shopping goods with few differences other than price are called homogeneous shopping goods.

T   2-21.   Advertisers usually wish to establish their products as heterogeneous shopping goods or as specialty goods.

F   2-22.   All specialty goods are luxury goods.

T   2-23.   An advertised product for which a customer will not accept a substitute is considered to be a specialty good.

T   2-24.   Every product is an unsought good at one point in its product life cycle.

T   2-25.   Advertisers of regularly unsought goods generally play on the consumer's emotions as they implant the idea of need in the consumer's mind for later development by a salesperson.

F   2-26.   The advertiser of an industrial building installation can generally expect a sale as a result of his advertising efforts.

F   2-27.   The terms "component parts" and "raw materials" can be used interchangeably as names for a type of business product.

F   2-28.   A product's image or personality can be improved upon in a short amount of time by an advertiser.

T   2-29.   An ad's physical appearance as well as its placement can affect the personality of a product.

F   2-30.   The life style for the market is the summation of all the demographic characteristics plus the market's attitudes.

Multiple Choice

C   2-31.   A target market is best defined as a:
A. Farm group
B. Business market group
C. Customer group upon which is placed primary marketing emphasis
D. Consumer market group
E. All of the above

E   2-32.   An advertiser would not ordinarily consider which of the following characteristics in determining a consumer target market:
A. Religious affiliation
B. Family income
C. Education
D. Occupation
E. Would consider all of the above

E   2-33.   The product aspect of the marketing mix includes which of the following?
A. Image
B. Services
C. What the customer buys from a firm
D. Goods
E. All of the above

70

D   2-34. All of the following characteristics of an advertisement directly affect a
            product's image except:
            A.   Ad placement
            B.   Ad copy
            C.   Ad layout
            D.   Ad cost
            E.   None of the above

A   2-35. Which of the following is not a common category of consumer goods?
            A.   Component goods
            B.   Shopping goods
            C.   Unsought goods
            D.   Specialty goods
            E.   Convenience goods

B   2-36   All the following are true statements about personality or image except:
            A.   The image is an important part of the marketing mix.
            B.   The image of a product is always different for every person.
            C.   The image must be developed over time.
            D.   The image is how the product/company is perceived by the consumer.
            E.   The image is created by product, place, price, and promotion.

C   2-37   Which of the following is not normally classified as a staple convenience
            good?
            A.   Eggs
            B.   Bread
            C.   Chicken
            D.   Milk
            E.   None of the above

E   3-28   Of the following examples, which is not normally classified as an impulse
            good?
            A.   Mints
            B.   Encyclopedias
            C.   Chewing gum
            D.   Life insurance
            E.   Both B and D

C   2-39   From an historical standpoint, an advertiser has not created a "new market"
            in which of the following advertisements?
            A.   Pick-up trucks for city slickers
            B.   Men's hair spray
            C.   "Secret" deodorant for women
            D.   Laundry detergent for singles
            E.   None of the above

B   2-40. An acceptable marketing mix contains all of the following except:
            A.   Place
            B.   Punctuality
            C.   Advertising, personal selling, and sales promotion
            D.   Good/service
            E.   Personality

B   2-41. All of the following are business market types except:
          A. Industrial
          B. Farm
          C. Professional
          D. Trade
          E. Institutional

A   2-42. All of the following are examples of industrial products advertised in the
          business market except:
          A. Mustard for a restaurant
          B. Ball bearings for roller skates
          C. Zippers for garment manufacturers
          D. Fuel pumps for farm tractors
          E. None of the above

E   2-43. A possible target market for an advertiser promoting an institutional product
          is:
          A. City hospitals
          B. Motels in Nashville, Tennessee
          C. College food services
          D. Kansas City restaurants
          E. All of the above

E   2-44. The farm market would not be the target market for which of the following
          goods/services?
          A. Machine shed
          B. John Deere tractor
          C. Firestone tires
          D. Local Restaurant
          E. All of the above could be related to the farm market

B   2-45. Which of the following advertisers does not understand the basic
          characteristics of consumers?
          A. Promoting hearing aids in a monthly newsletter for retired persons
          B. Promoting a Rolls Royce in a small town newspaper
          C. Promoting stock broker services in The Wall Street Journal
          D. Promoting Avis Rent-a-Cars in an airport lobby
          E. Promoting bagels in a predominantly Jewish neighborhood

E   2-46. An advertiser who thinks in terms of the marketing concept would not be
          customer-oriented in his:
          A. Actions
          B. Plans
          C. Procedures
          D. Policies
          E. None of the above is the best answer

D   2-47. Which of the following advertisements show an understanding of a consumer's
          life style?
          A. Millie, the company president, drinks Sanka coffee her secretary prepared.
          B. Arnold Palmer bought his wife a microwave oven so she would have more
              time to play golf with him.
          C. Irish Spring is used by males and females.
          D. Only two of the above
          E. All of the above

C 2-48. Which of the following markets advertises heavily in order to give away
its product free of charge in the hopes of a product endorsement?
A. Institutional
B. Raw material
C. Professional
D. Supplies
E. None of the above

A 2-49. Which of the following is not a heterogeneous shopping good?
A. Fresh corn in produce department
B. Oldsmobile from White's car dealer
C. Cannon towels
D. Milliken carpets
E. Act III clothes

D 2-50. The most popular reason why people buy is:
A. Brand loyalty
B. Snob appeal
C. Desire to be different
D. All of the above are popular reasons
E. None of the above are popular reasons

Completion

2-51. A company with customer-oriented plans, policies, procedures, and actions
is said to be following the (marketing concept).

2-52. A business firm that advertises a product to its target market while it
gives away the product to its target market is said to be selling to the
(professional) market.

2-53. A retailer learns about products through (trade) advertisements that tell
where consumer ads are running, how the product can be marketed, and/or
how the retailer can take part in promotional programs for the product.

2-54. A (convenience) good is an item that is purchased on a recurring basis, is
relatively inexpensive, or is dependent upon place availability for purchase.

2-55. One convenience good category consists of (staple) goods such as bread and
milk.

2-56. The key element in an advertisement for an emergency good is product
(availability).

2-57. (Homogeneous) shopping goods are only distinguished by price differences
while (heterogeneous) shopping goods have many differences.

2-58. A/an (target market) is those customers on whom the advertiser places primary
emphasis in developing the advertising program.

2-59. A proper (marketing mix) includes the following components: product, price,
place, promotion, and personality.

2-60. If a consumer will accept no substitute for a product, the advertiser has achieved the goal of making that product a (*specialty*) good in the consumer's eye.

CHAPTER 3 - EXTERNAL ADVERTISING RESTRAINTS

True or False

T   3-1. In 1914, Congress set up the Federal Trade Commission in an attempt to curb unfair competitive practices in the marketplace.

T   3-2. The Wheeler-Lea Amendment to the FTC Act reflected a change of emphasis in legislation from "a business must be harmed" to "a consumer must be harmed."

T   3-3. The Wheeler-Lea Amendment is often referred to as the "Truth in Advertising Act" because it deals with deceptive advertising.

T   3-4. According to the Wheeler-Lea Amendment, an ad that is misleading in a material respect either in what is stated or in what is purposely not revealed is a "false advertisement."

T   3-5. Two federal acts that are concerned with price discrimination in advertising are the "Magnuson-Moss Warranty-FTC Improvement Act" and the "Clayton Act."

T   3-6. One section of the Robinson-Patman Act requires equitable treatment concerning advertising discounts, rebates, allowances, or service charges for firms with like characteristics.

F   3-7. The "Truth in Advertising Act" requires the disclosure of all credit terms in an advertisement if any credit terms are disclosed.

F   3-8. The Federal Communications Commission is the only federal regulatory body that directly influences advertising.

T   3-9. Students Opposed to Unfair Practices (SOUP) was involved in the case against the Campbell Soup Company for use of marbles in its vegetable soup ads.

F   3-10. The Federal Trade Commission does not have the power to rule that a firm must run corrective ads at their own expense if they are found to have been using misleading ads in the past.

F   3-11. The practice of using a cheap item to attract customers to the store, and then telling them that the item is no longer available is called bait and tackle advertising.

F   3-12. Comparison advertising, the practice of comparing competing products, is illegal and unethical.

T   3-13. The advertising periodical, Printers' Ink, was continuously concerned with the problem of truth in advertising. Its Model Statute was adopted as law in 43 of the United States.

T   3-14. The Printers' Ink Model Statute was revised in 1959 to include fictitious comparative pricing and bait advertising.

F   3-15. The placement of advertising, such as outdoor signs, is generally regulated by federal law rather than by state or local law.

T   3-16. The advertising industry is attempting to regulate itself through the efforts of organizations like the Better Business Bureau.

F   3-17. The Better Business Bureau is a government agency that regulates the advertising industry.

T   3-18. Complaints to a local Better Business Bureau are evaluated to determine if there is any justification to them before the advertiser is requested to provide substantiating evidence.

T   3-19. If a firm refuses to change or discontinue its ad after a NARB panel has ruled that the ad is misleading, the case may be referred to a government agency for further action.

F   3-20. Since its creation in 1971, about one-half of the complaints to the Better Business Bureau have been successfully handled by the National Advertising Division (NAD) without the help of the FTC.

F   3-21. The radio and television media have not set many standards for their advertisers; they, instead, rely heavily on government regulations.

T   3-22. There is no one standard self-regulation code for magazine advertising.

F   3-23. The Television Code limits the amount of commercial time a station may use (sixteen minutes per hour during prime time).

T   3-24. The advertising industry is in part self-regulated through the efforts of the American Association of Advertising Agencies (AAAA) and the Association of National Advertisers (ANA).

F   3-25. Most advertisers have written regulations and codes to follow concerning the customs that may restrict advertising.

T   3-26. An awareness of Maslow's Hierarchy of needs may help explain to an advertiser what motivates people to act.

T   3-27. Advertisers should make an effort to learn about the elements of individual behavior (learning, attitudes, perceptions, and motives).

T   3-28. Much advertising success is due to repetition, one of the major tools of learning.

T   3-29. Advertisers often use existing attitudes to sell products, rather than trying to change consumer attitudes.

T   3-30. The family is an example of a reference group.

Multiple Choice

B   3-31.   In today's world of business, advertisers are faced with the task of creating
an advertising campaign that sells a product/service/idea while coping with
various external restraints. Which of the following is not considered to
be an external restraint?
A.   Customs
B.   Competition
C.   Consumer behavior
D.   Federal, state, and local laws and regulations
E.   All of the above are external restraints

C   3-32.   Among the numerous federal laws and regulations that affect advertising are
regulations covering which of the following topics:
   I.   Trademarks and their legal protection
  II.   Consumer need for safety; protection
 III.   Curbing unfair competition
  IV.   Advertisement placement
   V.   False advertisements
  VI.   Price discrimination

A.   I, II, V, VI
B.   I, III, IV, V
C.   I, III, V, VI
D.   III, IV, V, VI
E.   All of the above

E   3-33.   A definition of "false advertisement" would include all of the following
except:
A.   Failure to reveal relevant facts
B.   Suggestions made by ad's design
C.   Representations by sound and statement
D.   Misleading in a material respect
E.   All of the above are included

D   3-34.   The Printers' Ink Model Statute was revised in 1959 to include which of the
following:
A.   Bait advertising
B.   Intent
C.   Fictitious comparative pricing
D.   Only two of the above
E.   All of the above

A   3-35.   Which of the following ads would be least likely to be cited as a "false
advertisement" based on federal laws and regulations?
A.   A Chrysler ad comparing its small K-body car to the Chevrolet Citation
B.   An ad stating that Head and Shoulders shampoo is superior to Tegrin
C.   Men's cologne ad guaranteeing female companionship for the user
D.   An ad stating that Doan's Pills cure ailing livers
E.   All of the above are likely to be cited

E 3-36. When General Motors introduced their new "big cars" in 1977, they:
         A. Had to change the "small is bad" attitude
         B. Encouraged test drives
         C. Encountered cognitive dissonance
         D. Used informative advertising
         E. All of the above

A 3-37. Possible actions that could be taken on a complaint by NAD include all of the
         following except:
         A. Fines
         B. Evaluation
         C. Appeals
         D. Substantiation
         E. All of the above are possible actions

E 3-38. Consumer behavior would not be concerned with which of the following:
         A. Using economic goods and services
         B. Purchasing economic goods and services
         C. Planning economic goods and services
         D. Both B and C
         E. A, B, and C are all found to be a part of consumer behavior

C 3-39. According to Maslow's Hierarchy of Needs, which of the following needs would
         an advertiser be less likely to use as a primary motive for buying an
         automobile:
         A. Belonging
         B. Esteem
         C. Physiological
         D. Self-actualization
         E. All of the above could be used

B 3-40. The T.V. Code as established by the Television Review Board is not concerned
         with which of the following television problems:
         A. Liquor advertisements
         B. Content of programs
         C. Amount of commercial time per hour
         D. Content of advertisements
         E. None of the above are incorrect

E 3-41. The advertising industry's efforts at self-regulation include all of the
         following except:
         A. Media standards
         B. Better Business Bureau
         C. Advertising agency standards
         D. National Advertising Review Board
         E. All of the above are self-regulations

D 3-42. When considering individual behavior, a clothing advertiser would not be
         concerned with:
         A. Attitudes
         B. Motvies
         C. Perception
         D. Social class
         E. Learning

A 3-43. Which of the following class characteristics, according to Martineau, would
probably not be represented in an advertisement for a product that is
advertised to a middle class target market:
A. Family orientation
B. Self-confidence
C. Urban identification
D. Future orientation
E. Rational behavior

D 3-44. The lower status social class is characterized by:
A. Rural identity
B. Concern about security and insecurity
C. Unlimited or vastly extended horizons
D. Two of the above
E. All of the above

A 3-45. Which of the following statements concerning the National Advertising
Review Board is false?
A. NARB keeps its activities and actions private.
B. NARB reviews complaint appeals made by advertisers.
C. NARB was established by the Council of Better Business Bureaus.
D. NARB handled 30 cases in its first five years of existence.
E. All of the above are true.

C 3-46. As a result of Warner-Lambert's challenge to the Federal Trade Commission's
decision concerning their Listerine ads, they did not:
A. Go to court
B. Use the corrective statement: "Listerine will not help prevent colds or
or sore throats or lessen their severity."
C. Win the case
D. Spend $10 billion on corrective advertising
E. All of the above were done

E 3-47. Which of the following statements concerning perception is not true?
A. The color of a package can affect a consumer's perception of the product.
B. Perception is difficult to analyze because of individual differences.
C. Perception is affected by a consumer's needs.
D. Perception is an external advertising restraint.
E. All the above are true.

E 3-48. Advertisers may find that group behavior:
A. Affects buyer behavior
B. Is influenced by opinion leaders
C. Is difficult to separate from individual behavior
D. Is related to reference groups
E. All of the above

E 3-49. All of the following except one can cause subcultures that an advertiser needs
to be aware of:
A. Geography
B. National origin
C. Religion
D. Life-style
E. All of the above create subcultures

78

E   3-50. The Magnuson-Moss Warranty-Federal Trade Commision Improvement Act:
A. Expanded the number of FTC offices to 35
B. Eliminated the consent decree as a viable enforcement device
C. Concerned itself with stopping present practices in the market place
D. All of the above
E. None of the above

Completion

3-51. Advertisers need an understanding of (_consumer behavior_) or that behavior exhibited by people in planning, purchasing, and using economic goods and services.

3-52. In 1914, Congress set up the (_Federal Trade Commission_) to curb unfair competitive practices in the market place.

3-53. The Clayton Act and the Robinson-Patman Act are concerned with (_price discrimination_). They require equal promotional allowances for firms with like characteristics.

3-54   (_"Bait"_) advertising is a form of false advertising because it features a cheap item that isn't in stock to attract customers so that they can then be convinced to buy a more expensive model.

3-55. Customs are a restriction on advertising because a market's customs influence how people (_perceive_) or view the advertising that is presented to them.

3-56. A good advertiser makes an effort to learn about the psychological or (_individual_) behavior of a market's consumers as well as its group behavior and cultural makeup.

3-57. (_Learning_), or the change in response tendencies due to the effects of experience, is a key behavioral element that an advertiser can use to help remove consumer behavior as an external restraint to effective advertising.

3-58. The major learning tools that are used by advertisers are (_repetition_) and (_contiguity_).

3-59. Knowing (_opinion leaders_) or people who have obtained some unique distinction in others' minds, makes the task of selling a product easier.

3-60. A learned tendency to respond in a given manner to a particular situation is known as a/an (_attitude_).

CHAPTER 4 - THE ADVERTISING INDUSTRY

True or False

F   4-1. "Advertising Agency" is another name for a company's advertising department.

T   4-2. In many firms, an advertising department may consist of one person.

T   4-3. Even a one-person advertising department should plan its advertising program.

F 4-4. An "in-house" agency is in reality just an advertising department.

T 4-5. A one-person advertising department can succeed if planning and coordination are carried out.

T 4-6. In many cases, an advertiser allows the media to determine the advertising program, develop the ads, and present the ads to the target market.

F 4-7. Special service groups were originally started to aid the media with the art work.

F 4-8. Of the approximately 6,000 advertising agencies in the United States, two-thirds are "one-man" shops.

F 4-9. The media representative, not the advertiser, should decide if a particular ad should be run and what the copy should be.

T 4-10. The most widely used form of advertising service groups are found in printing.

F 4-11. The media's only function is to serve as a vehicle for carrying an advertising message.

T 4-12. Both primary and secondary research are used in seeking the information necessary to develop a good advertising program.

T 4-13. A full-service agency determines the present and potential market through research, ingenuity, and experience.

F 4-14. A good advertiser strives to use the media which will carry his message to the greatest number of people no matter what the cost.

F 4-15. Size is the main determinant of success for an advertising department or advertising agency.

T 4-16. The full-service agency is held completely responsible for an ad's success or failure whereas the media are not.

F 4-17. An ad agency should be more interested in turning out creative work than in successfully promoting the clients products.

F 4-18. A full-service agency is generally more expensive because of its piecemeal manner of completing a campaign.

F 4-19. Advertising agencies are paid from fees, commissions, and kick-backs.

T 4-20. Position titles in an ad agency may not reflect the relative position of the person in the agency structure.

T 4-21. A substantial portion of overall advertising agency income is obtained through commissions.

F 4-22. Even when commissions for an advertising agency are large, charges for various extra services are typically passed on to the client at a cost of 20%.

F   4-23. A brand or product manager is held accountable (in the functional sense) for only the advertising of the product.

F   4-24. In 1956, the Justice Department ruled that the agency commission recognition requirements were legal as an industry practice, but illegal for individual firms within the industry.

T   4-25. In the full-service advertising department, the advertiser and the "agency" are under the same top management.

T   4-26. Coordination is a major problem whenever an advertising agency is created by using various service groups.

T   4-27. Media representatives usually lack the objectivity and expertise needed to develop a good advertising plan for a firm.

T   4-28. Every firm needs to make a careful analysis of the alternatives available with respect to the advertising plan to insure that a wise choice is made.

T   4-29. The organizational structure of an advertising department can be divided by products, customers, geographic regions, or advertising functions.

F   4-30. A firm who uses an advertising agency has no need for an advertising department.

Multiple Choice

D   4-31. Which of the following is not a distinct part of the advertising industry?
         A. Media
         B. Special service groups
         C. Advertising department
         D. Marketing research department
         E. All of the above are included

D   4-32. The advertising department of a firm:
         A. Varies in its placement in the organizational structure
         B. Varies in size and scope depending on the importance of advertising
         C. Should be set up by product group
         D. Two of the above are correct
         E. All of the above are correct

D   4-33. An "in-house" advertising agency:
         A. Has no clients other than the parent company and its subsidiaries
         B. Allows the advertising department to receive commissions
         C. Is owned completely by the advertiser
         D. Two of the above are correct
         D. All of the above are correct

E   4-34. Which of the following would be considered a disadvantage of using an advertising department as opposed to an advertising agency?
         A. Complete advertising control
         B. Inexpensive
         C. The department personnel work for the company
         D. Two of the above are disadvantages
         E. None of the above

E 4-35. Which of the following are service standards as set forth by the American
        Association of Advertising Agencies for use in full-service advertising
        agencies?
                I.   Understanding distribution
               II.   Product study
              III.   Plan implementation
               IV.   Plan formulation
                V.   Publicity and public relations assistance
               VI.   Potential market study

            A. I, III, IV, VI
            B. I, II, III, VI
            C. II, III, IV, V
            D. I, II, V, VI
            E. All of the above

B 4-36. Which of the following would not be included in an advertising department
        that is divided by functional areas?
            A. Selection of media
            B. Geographic location
            C. Actual making of the ads
            D. Creation of ads
            E. Analysis of products, markets, and media

C 4-37. The advertising plan that an agency gives to its client should make
        recommendations on all the following except:
            A. What advertising messages should be used
            B. Appeals to be used
            C. What ad colors should be used
            D. Markets to be reached
            E. Distribution changes, if any

C 4-38. Special service advertising groups are available to provide all the
        following except:
            A. Stuntmen
            B. Radio jingles
            C. Advertising campaigns
            D. Artwork
            E. All of the above are correct

B 4-39. A full service advertising agency would probably not assist its client in
        a non-advertising area such as:
            A. Sales literature
            B. Management of sales
            C. Public relations
            D. Package design
            E. All of the above

A 4-40. The organizational structure of an advertising agency is usually not:
            A. Divided into product groups
            B. Designed to have its account executives on the same level as their
                clients, "titlewise."
            C. Designed to work in a functional manner
            D. Divided into creative, account, marketing services, and operations
                management
            E. All of the above are correct

D   4-41. Under a fee system of compensation, the agency:
          A. Is not tempted to recommend using media with higher commissions
          B. Sets fees on noncommissioned media
          C. Rebates all commissions to the client
          D. A and C are correct
          E. A, B and C are correct

C   4-42. Important factors in selecting an advertising agency include all of the
          following except:
          A. Specialization requirements
          B. Size of the agency
          C. Number of photographers employed
          D. Experience
          E. Competitive accounts handled

B   4-43. Advertising agencies are normally compensated by means of all the following
          methods except:
          A. Fees
          B. Royalties
          C. Charges
          D. Commissions
          E. All of the above

A   4-44. Which of the following is not true about most media representatives?
          A. Have extensive advertising training
          B. Create ad copy
          C. Sell ad space
          D. All of the above are true
          E. None of the above are true

A   4-45. Which of the following is not a problem that must be faced by a one-person
          advertising department:
          A. Failure is just a matter of time due to its size
          B. Labor specialization is nonexistent
          C. The person handling advertising normally has many other responsibilities
          D. Time is short
          E. All of the above are problems

E   4-46. Major reasons for using a full-service agency include:
              I. Synergistic experience
             II. Greater objectivity
            III. Simplified coordination
             IV. Centralization of authority and responsibility
              V. More talent
             VI. May be less expensive

          A. I, III, V, VI
          B. I, II, V, VI
          C. II, III, IV, V, VI
          D. I, II, III, IV, V, VI
          E. I, II, III, IV, V, VI, and others

E   4-47. An understanding of the factors of distribution by a full-service
            advertising agency:
            A. Requires that the agency learn the distribution system of each client
            B. Provides advice on how to get the product profitably to the point of sale
            C. Includes ideas beyond the scope of advertising
            D. Explains why many agencies specialize in certain industries
            E. All of the above

E   4-48. An advertising agency's knowledge of the media does not have to include an
            understanding of:
            A. Media cost
            B. Media audience
            C. Media market
            D. Character and influence of the media
            E. All of the above are important

A   4-49. Which of the following statements concerning advertising agency commissions
            is false?
            A. Outdoor advertising provides a lower commission than most media.
            B. All media do not quote a commission rate.
            C. A substantial portion of agency income is obtained through commissions.
            D. Most media provide a 15% commission to the agency.
            E. All of the above are true.

C   4-50. If an advertising agency buys $2 million worth of television advertising with
            a 15 percent commission and a 2 percent cash discount, what should the
            agency pay the media and bill the client?
            A. $1,700,000, $2,000,000
            B. $1,715,000, $2,000,000
            C. $1,666,000, $1,966,000
            D. $1,700,000, $1,966,000
            E. None of the above

Completion

4-51. The advertising industry is made up of the following four divisions:
       (*special service groups*), (*advertising departments*), (*media*), and
       (*advertising agencies*).

4-52. The product or (*brand*) manager concept as used by Procter & Gamble and
       General Foods holds the manager accountable for the advertising and marketing
       of a product.

4-53. A (*full-service*) advertising department performs all the functions necessary
       to develop and implement an advertising program.

4-54. (*Advertising agency*) is defined as an organization of business and creative
       people who are dedicated to making advertising succeed.

4-55. An agency is said to be recognized if it meets what criteria:
       (*independent of any advertiser/media*), (*financially sound*), and
       (*capable personnel*).

4-56. An (*in-house agency*) is an arrangement where an advertising agency is
       owned completely by the advertiser.

84

4-57. The organizational structure for an advertising agency relies heavily on (_functional_) authority as the account executive acts as the liaison with the client.

4-58. Though an advertising agency receives as 15 percent commission for placing an ad in most media, outdoor advertising provides a (_16 2/3_)% commission.

4-59. The (_fee system_) of compensation could promote a more professional atmosphere in the agency business, since the agency receives the same compensation regardless of the media selected for use.

4-60. An "in-house" advertising department would seek the help of a (_special service group_) when their advertising needs call for something out of the ordinary.

CHAPTER 5 - ADVERTISING FOUNDATION

True or False

T   5-1. If any of the components of the communication process are wrong (advertisement, media, etc.), then the communication process will fail.

T   5-2. In many instances, media firms develop market studies for the purpose of showing the advertiser that he/she should use that media.

F   5-3. The Census of Wholesale Trade and the Census of Manufacturers are market analysis reports that are supplied by trade associations.

T   5-4. Firms that are regulated by the government or that do business with the government must reveal certain information which may be of use to competing advertisers.

T   5-5. One of the steps in market analysis is the evaluation of how much of the market, if any, is served by the competition.

T   5-6. The true test of uniqueness for a product is determined by the target market, not the advertiser.

F   5-7. Advertisers know that children have little influence on their parents' purchase decisions.

F   5-8. From a legal standpoint, trademarks must always be affixed to the product.

T   5-9. It is difficult to use the dictionary as a trademark source because you should avoid words that define or describe the product.

T   5-10. Historically, the use of a personal name as a trademark has included names of real persons, fictional persons, and historical persons.

F   5-11. From a legal standpoint, geographic and/or personal names are good sources for a trademark for a new product.

T   5-12. A brand name can also be a trade name if it names the product as well as the company.

F 5-13. In order for a service mark to be registered with the Library of Congress it must be used in international trade.

T 5-14. Since most customers do not separate the package from the product, the package is part of product analysis.

T 5-15. Some advertisers successfully promote and sell their products to two distinct markets, while using the same package for both markets.

F 5-16. Advertisers are concerned about legal requirements such as the placement of the Universal Package Code (U.P.C.) on the package.

T 5-17. A firm that changes an existing package hopes that potential customers will see and try the product while present users will continue to use or increase their usage of the product.

T 5-18. Changing the package for an existing product is risky as many loyal users may think the product itself is also changed.

F 5-19. As of 1980, there have not been any companies that have attempted to develop an advertising strategy that will position a product in such a way as to create a new market segment.

T 5-20. All advertising strategies must insure that primary demand is present.

F 5-21. A product's advertising strategy will shift toward primary demand as competition enters the market and customers learn the merits of a product.

T 5-22. Marketing directly to the consumer market is an effective but expensive advertising strategy.

T 5-23. Many firms successfully use both product advertising and institutional advertising in promoting their products.

T 5-24. Customers who can be shown how to use a product more by means of advertising can become better customers.

F 5-25. Business firms are just beginning to use advertising to change habits as well as thinking.

T 5-26. Advertising is used as an ice breaker for many business situations.

T 5-27. Advertising is sometimes used to obtain sales leads for a product or service.

F 5-28. "To increase sales" is always the best advertising objective for an advertiser.

T 5-29. The Lanham Act deals with the use of trademarks.

F 5-30. More firms use a "pull" advertising strategy than any other advertising approach.

86

Multiple Choice

D   5-31. The communication process as it applies to advertising is a closed loop
          system that includes all the following except:
          A. Advertising media
          B. Advertiser
          C. Customer
          D. Verbal message
          E. Behavior effect

B   5-32. Relatively current data on the "total market" for a product are found in all
          the following sources except:
          A. Government documents
          B. Marketing textbooks
          C. Trade publications
          D. Media
          E. Trade associations

A   5-33. Which of the following is not an example of market data information that
          you would normally find in trade publications?
          A. Census data
          B. Buying potential for a city or county
          C. Sales estimates for products
          D. Information on a particular industry
          E. All the above are found in trade journals

E   5-34. In order for the advertiser to conduct a market analysis, information is
          needed on the:
          A. Competition
          B. Package
          C. Total market
          D. A, B and C are correct
          E. A and C are correct

A   5-35. Which of the following statements concerning product analysis is false?
          A. It determines who influences the purchase decision.
          B. The end result is an advertiser who is better informed about the product.
          C. It evaluates the product's package and physical characteristics.
          D. It may cause product improvements.
          E. All the above are true.

E   5-36. A firm could use which of the following as a means of identifying the item
          to be advertised.
          A. Brand
          B. Slogan
          C. Trade character
          D. Service mark
          E. All of the above

A   5-37. Legally a trademark must be:
          A. Attached to the product or product container
          B. Deceptive
          C. Applied for before the product is sold in interstate trade
          D. A coined or dictionary word
          E. Descriptive

D 5-38. Common sources of trademarks include which of the following?
         I.   Researchers   IV. Dictionary
         II. Coined word   V.   School teachers
         III. Geographical name   VI. Licensed name

         A. I, III, IV, VI
         B. II, III, V, VI
         C. I, II, III, VI
         D. II, III, IV, VI
         E. I, II, IV, VI

D 5-39. Advertisers of generic products, such as <u>Kleenex</u> facial tissue and <u>Scotch</u>
         tape, should check their advertising procedures to insure that the trademark:
         A. Is not used in a plural sense (to take the place of a generic name)
         B. Is distinctive in all ads
         C. Modifies the generic name for the product
         D. All of the above
         E. None of the above

B 5-40. In making a product analysis, an advertiser should be aware of the
         characteristics of all the following brand types he is dealing with except:
         A. Private
         B. Homemade
         C. Individual
         D. National
         E. Family

A 5-41. All of the following are family brands except:
         A. Coca Cola
         B. Hunt's
         C. Del Monte
         D. Heinz
         E. All the above are family brands

D 5-42. Advertisers have learned that people are attracted to branded products
         because:
         A. They give prestige
         B. They are guaranteed
         C. They are familiar
         D. Only A and C
         E. All the above

C 5-43. In trying to develop a good slogan, an advertiser should not:
         A. Generate interest
         B. Set the product/service/idea apart in some way
         C. Cause confusion
         D. Offer or imply a reward
         E. None of the above

B 5-44. If used in an advertising campaign, a trade character should not:
         A. Be updated or modified
         B. Detract from the product
         C. Help sell the product/service/idea
         D. Provide continuity
         E. Generate interest for a particular advertising program

⑩ E 5-45. The promotional function of a product's package is important to the
            advertiser for the following reason(s):
            A. The use of a reusable glass or jar often encourages sales
            B. A promotional package may make a product obsolete
            C. A product is often purchased because of its package
            D. Only B and C
            E. All the above

B 5-46. All the following are questions advertisers need to answer about a product's
          physical characteristics except:
          A. What does the product do?
          B. Where was the product designed?
          C. What makes the product unique?
          D. How is the product made?
          E. None of the above

C. 5-47. Armed with the market analysis and the product analysis, the advertiser
           is now better prepared to choose an advertising strategy from any of the
           following except:
           A. Push demand vs. pull demand
           B. Institutional advertising vs. product advertising
           C. Primary demand vs. secondary demand
           D. Total market vs. market segment
           E. All the above are likely strategies

C 5-48. Which of the following statements about institutional advertising is false?
          A. It should not replace product advertising.
          B. It should not be used too extensively.
          C. It should always be used by an advertiser.
          D. It uses money from the product advertising budget.
          E. All the above are true.

E 5-49. Which of the following is not a possible objective of a specific advertising
          campaign?
          A. Confirm imagery
          B. Change habits
          C. Induce trial
          D. Generate sales leads
          E. All the above are possible objectives

D 5-50. According to James I. Bernadin, all the following are ways for the advertiser
          to achieve the goal of a good advertising foundation except:
          A. Study the marketing plan.
          B. Understand the assignment before you start.
          C. Understand the advertising problem before you write anything.
          D. Decide how to say it before you decide what you want to say.
          E. All the above are ways.

Completion

5-51. Any word, name, symbol, or device used by a manufacturer or merchant to
       identify his goods and distinguish them from those manufactured or sold by
       others is a (*trademark*).

5-52. The "trademark" of a firm advertising a service rather than a product is called a/an (*service mark*).

5-53. A firm often uses a/an (*trade character*), such as Betty Crocker, to obtain continuity in various ads for the product over time.

5-54. Advertisers recognize that a package serves two functions: (*protection*) and (*promotion*).

5-55. The ultimate test of product uniqueness is in the eyes of the (*target market*), not the advertiser.

5-56. An advertiser is using a (*total market*) advertising strategy when he sells a product as a mass commodity, and a (*market segment*) advertising strategy when he sells to a clearly defined market.

5-57. The advertisements for an entirely new product must create (*primary*) demand for the product as well as brand awareness.

5-58. A/an (*push demand*) strategy is being used when the merits of a product are advertised to the marketing channel in hopes of getting the product carried and promoted by the store. On the other hand, the manufacturer that goes directly to the customer with the advertising program is using a/an (*pull demand*) strategy.

5-59. Firms who advertise numerous products while working to build the total product line as opposed to just advertising a specific item alone, are following the objective of (*building line acceptance*).

5-60. (*Ambience*), the positive feeling about a business that advertising helps create, can mean long term success only if there is actually a positive environment within the firm.

CHAPTER 6 - ADVERTISING COPYWRITING

True or False

T 6-1. USP stands for Unique Selling Proposition.

F 6-2. In all cases, a creative advertisement is thought to be a good advertisement.

T 6-3. A good copywriter studies the answers to questions asked about the product and the market because he knows they are essential to the creation of successful ads.

T 6-4. Every advertisement should try to sell a specific benefit to the prospect.

F 6-5. The smart advertiser determines what is unique about a product without considering the target market.

F 6-6. A good advertisement concentrates on product characteristics.

F 6-7. A person in the awareness stage of the adoption process searches for information about the product.

F   6-8.   A copywriter can assume that all recipients of an ad message for an established product already have product awareness.

T   6-9.   A good copy platform is the summation of much work on the part of the copywriter.

F   6-10.   Humorous commercials always sell products.

T   6-11.   A straight-sell advertisement normally includes a call for action.

T   6-12.   Many slice-of-life commercials are unrealistic dramatizations, but are still considered to be good commercials because consumers can identify with them in some way.

F   6-13.   The use of verse seldom pays off with good advertising results.

F   6-14.   The educational copy format is seldom used in institutional advertisements.

F   6-15.   The primary purpose of ad copy is to get the attention of the target market.

T   6-16.   The unique selling proposition for a product might be used to help create interest by pointing out benefits to buyers.

T   6-17.   A headline issuing a command can be an effective attention-getting advertisement.

F   6-18.   A sub-headline is required to make the transition from the headline to the copy.

F   6-19.   Consumer advertisements rely heavily on rational reasons for the purchase of a product/service/idea.

T   6-20.   The closing segment of an advertisement should include a call for action that considers the selling approach as well as the passive points.

F   6-21.   Information that may be pertinent to the ad, but that is passive in that it does not play a major role in ad creation, can usually be deleted from the ad without causing any problems.

T   6-22.   It is not enough for an ad to be true...the target market must believe that the ad is true.

F   6-23.   Simplicity in advertising connotes short, basic copy.

T   6-24.   The use of readability measurements like the Gunning Fog Index penalize the writer for using long sentences and polysyllabic words.

T   6-25.   Cliches and superlatives should be used if they make good, effective advertising copy.

T   6-26.   A copywriter should learn as much as possible about the target market so as to avoid using words with negative connotations in the ads.

T   6-27.   Copywriters should try to be brief while being specific.

F 6-28. The first rule of message adaptation is "Know thy self."

F 6-29. If a copywriter has a personal dislike for an ad in its finished form, the copy should not be used.

T 6-30. Understanding each part of the copy structure and how they relate to each other is essential to good copywriting.

Multiple Choice

C 6-31. The basic ingredients of good copywriting include all the following except:
   A. Style
   B. Thinking
   C. Punctuation
   D. Structure
   E. All of the above are included

B 6-32. Copy thinking should include all the following elements except:
   A. Development of the U.S.P.
   B. Determination of K.I.S.S.
   C. Consideration of the adoption process
   D. Information about the product and market
   E. All of the above

D 6-33. In which of the following stages in the adoption process for an item being advertised may customers be found?
I.	Trial	IV.	Interest
II.	Rejection	V.	Post adoption
III.	Education	VI.	Awareness

   A. I, III, IV, V
   B. III, IV, V, VI
   C. I, II, IV, VI
   D. I, IV, V, VI
   E. All of the above

A 6-34. Which of the following statements concerning testimonial copy formats is false?
   A. From a practical standpoint, testimonial advertising is limited to the consumer market.
   B. The testimonial ad should be believable.
   C. Testimonial ads are effective in selling to the farm market.
   D. Good testimonial ads are difficult to develop.
   E. None of the above

E 6-35. The cartoon format in an advertisement is never:
   A. Serious in nature
   B. Effective in obtaining readership
   C. Developed into a continuing story over time
   D. The cause for a loss in credibility
   E. None of the above

92

B   6-36. The educational copy format is used for all the following reasons except:
A.   To raise questions of reader interest
B.   To determine the market's education level
C.   To create primary demand for a product
D.   To inform readers about the institution
E.   None of the above

C   6-37. A well-structured advertisement would include all the following except:
A.   Action
B.   Interest
C.   Determination
D.   Attention
E.   All of the above are included

E   6-38. A headline can get the attention of the target market by all the following techniques except:
A.   Raising a question
B.   Stressing a benefit
C.   Stating some news
D.   Arousing curiosity
E.   All of the above are correct

A   6-39. Which of the following advertising headlines would be the least effective attention-getter?
A.   "Gordy's salt is perfect for removing snow and ice, and for making ice cream."
B.   "A special service now offered for those 21-25 years old."
C.   "Buy before December 23 and save."
D.   "There are more raisins in Post Raisin Bran."
E.   "Would you deny a child food?"

C   6-40. The body of an advertisement should not:
A.   Include the important elements of the copy platform
B.   Provide subjective and objective reasons for purchase
C.   Have a specific limit to the number of facts
D.   Attempt to sell
E.   Convey an image of positive value

A   6-41. Which of the following is not generally thought to be of the soft-sell approach in closing an advertisement:
A.   Informs the customer when the sale/special ends
B.   Requests that a customer remember the product name/service and hopefully buy at a future date.
C.   Refers to ads that promote "indirect action"
D.   Shows the emotional aspect of a product as a reason for future purchase
E.   All of the above

E   6-42. In developing good copy style, a copywriter should consider which of the following points?
A.   Readability
B.   K.I.S.S.
C.   Believability
D.   Both A and C
E.   All of the above

A 6-43. Which of the following statements about simplicity in advertising is false?
A. Simple copy means short copy.
B. The copy should be easy reading for the customer group.
C. Copywriters should try to keep the copy sweet and simple.
D. Simple messages can be effective advertisements.
E. The copy may include terminology which is used by the target group.

C 6-44. A copywriter enhances readability by using all the following except:
A. Personal pronouns in second person
B. Contractions in conversational copy
C. Passive voice for smooth readability and listening
D. Familiar words known to the market
E. Few punctuation marks

E 6-45. In determining the word count for an advertisement, the copywriter would probably not consider:
A. The objective of the ad
B. The space and time available
C. The complexity of the message in relation to the target market
D. The type of product advertised
E. Should consider all of the above

C 6-46. Which of the following examples would be most characteristic of copy thinking when using a well developed U.S.P?
A. Detergent A gets out ordinary dirt
B. Toothpaste B contains flouride
C. Car C gives the smooth ride of a luxury car at an economy car price
D. Cereal D is sugar-coated
E. None of the above

D 6-47. Which of the following statements is not true about a unique selling proposition?
A. An ad's purpose is to promote a product/service/idea.
B. Product uniqueness depends on the target market's wants.
C. The proposition must be important enough to cause consumers to switch brands.
D. A proposition need not be beneficial so long as it is unique.
E. None of the above

A 6-48. A copy platform normally includes all the following points except:
A. Desired copy layout and design
B. Desired initial and future behavior of the prospect
C. Verbal and visual advertising approaches
D. Product benefits
E. Quality features and workmanship

B 6-49. All of the following are commonly used copy formats except:
A. Slice-of-life
B. Question
C. Humorous
D. News
E. Verse

E 6-50. Which of the following points should be considered in the closing segment of the advertisement?
A. The store/company logo
B. The selling approach
C. The legal passive points
D. Both B and C
E. All the above

Completion

6-51. The person who writes advertising copy is known as the (*copywriter*).

6-52. The elements of copy structure include (*headline*), (*body*), and (*close*).

6-53. A person who is in the (*trial*) stage of the adoption process may buy or test the item being advertised depending on its cost.

6-54. A copy format that places the buyer's benefits before the market in a matter-of-fact, to-the-point manner is the (*straight-sell*) format.

6-55. The dramatization advertisement or the (*slice-of-life*) format is a straight-sell format placed within a particular atmosphere for a desired effect.

6-56. Since the (*news*) ad format gives the impression of being a part of the editorial copy of the magazine or newspaper, it obtains high readership.

6-57. Advertisements structured with the AIDA formula in mind focus on (*attention*), (*interest*), (*desire*), and (*action*) within the ad.

6-58. An advertisement that tells a customer in the closing section of the ad that he must act now is using a (*hard-sell*) approach.

6-59. The Gunning Fog Index is one system that can be used by copywriters to measure (*readability*).

6-60. When calculating the Gunning Fog Index, an index of (*12*) will be found if the average sentence length is twelve words and the number of polysyllables in the sample is 18 words.

CHAPTER 7 - ADVERTISING PRESENTATION

True or False

F 7-1. A given ad in an advertising campaign usually has two layouts created for study during the planning phase.

T 7-2. Advertisers may choose to go directly from the rough layout to a finished ad in order to avoid the expense of the comprehensive layout.

T 7-3. A storyboard for a television ad may or may not include acting and camera directions.

F 7-4. An asymmetrical layout tends to give the feeling of dignity, security, and dependability.

T   7-5.   A new product may be more effectively advertised by the use of an informally balanced ad.

T   7-6.   The direction of eye movement for an ad will vary depending on the culture of the area where the advertisement is run.

F   7-7.   To achieve adequate attention value, equal space should be given to all components of an advertisement.

F   7-8.   The impact of a particular contrast technique will not diminish over time provided that another advertiser does not adopt the same approach.

F   7-9.   There is a direct conflict between the layout principles of unity and contrast. The advertiser must decide which one will be applied to the situation.

T   7-10.   The principle that works to insure that each ad for a campaign as well as all the ads together appear as a single unit is unity.

F   7-11.   Readers of advertising copy generally look for conceptual proportional alignment in an ad.

F   7-12.   Contrast is of little importance when an ad is surrounded by other ads in its environment.

T   7-13.   The advertising message consists of art work and/or copy.

T   7-14.   The repetition of an ad featuring the product itself may lead to a high product recognition level among customers.

F   7-15.   It is always desirable for an advertiser to show his product in use in an advertisement.

T   7-16.   The use of too many features in one ad will diminish the impact of each feature on the target market.

F   7-17.   Two product features can usually be presented effectively in a ten-second commercial.

T   7-18.   An advertiser who is attempting to show movement in print media can create that feeling through the use of artwork.

F   7-19.   Drawings are the most effective form of artwork when realism is desired.

T   7-20.   A line drawing can be used by an advertiser to convey quality, illustrate a product benefit, or present an idea.

T   7-21.   Line drawings offer consistency of appearance when more than one product is shown in an ad.

T   7-22.   The only limits on the use of diagrams in advertisements are legal restraints and the creativity of the art director.

F   7-23.   In the United States, the color orange represents a cool, refreshing, and peaceful mood.

F   7-24.   The task of color selection is made easy since colors have the same meaning
             for everyone.

T   7-25.   Color in an advertisement can be a powerful communicator.

F   7-26.   Shades of the same color can be used effectively in an ad that is shown
             on television.

T   7-27.   A basic color is called a hue.

F   7-28.   Chroma is defined as the lightness or darkness of the hue.

F   7-29.   The strength or weakness of a color is determined by its value.

T   7-30.   The balance of an ad is affected by the size of illustrations, the
             arrangement of copy, and the use of color.

Multiple Choice

A   7-31.   Which of the following is not a stage or type of layout found in most forms
             of print advertising?
             A.   Storyboard
             B.   Comprehensive layout
             C.   Thought sketch
             D.   Mechanical layout
             E.   Rough layout

B   7-32.   Which of the following is not the name of a layout principle:
             A.   Movement
             B.   Placement
             C.   Proportion
             D.   Unity
             E.   Balance

D   7-33.   The principle of balance is characterized by all of the following except:
             A.   Color usage affects balance
             B.   Illustration size affects balance
             C.   Formal balance gives a feeling of dignity
             D.   Good balance makes a person see more of the ad
             E.   None of the above

A   7-34.   Which of the following is not a characteristic of the principle of ad
             proportion:
             A.   Ad copy that exceeds 50 characters per line is common in a well-
                  proportioned ad
             B.   Proportion is related to balance and movement
             C.   Proportion requires the layout designer to determine the importance
                  of various components
             D.   Ad copy that is divided into columns may improve an ad's effectiveness
             E.   None of the above

C   7-35.   Which of the following statements concerning the contrast principle is
            false?
            A.   The advertiser should choose a contrast technique that is not being
                 used in the area.
            B.   Contrast is used to make someone take notice.
            C.   Contrast is seldom achieved by using an unusual border around the ad.
            D.   Contrast makes the important elements of an ad stand out.
            E.   Effective attention-getting is a never ending task for the advertiser.

B   7-36.   If the unity design principle is being used by an advertiser, then:
            A.   White space cannot be used in an ad
            B.   All elements of each ad should work together
            C.   Contrast will not be used
            D.   Both A and B
            E.   All of the above

E   7-37.   The layout environment is important because:
            A.   Ad movement on a billboard may direct a person's eye to a neighboring ad
            B.   Television ads compete with one another as they run together
            C.   A two-page magazine ad may not match perfectly
            D.   An ad having a unique personality in its environment will be remembered
            E.   All of the above

E   7-38.   In terms of the role of artwork in an advertisement, art can be used to show:
              I.   Specific product features   IV.   Product in use
             II.   Supplemental information   V.   Product being tested
            III.   Action   VI.   Product itself

            A.   II, III, IV, V
            B.   II, III, IV, VI
            C.   I, III, IV, V
            D.   I, III, IV, VI
            E.   All of the above

E   7-39.   A product test can be effective if:
            A.   Careful thought is used to develop the ad
            B.   The facts can be substantiated in the ad
            C.   The ad does not just inform the customer of the competition
            D.   Only B and C
            E.   All the above

E   7-40.   Artwork may be used in an ad to provide which of the following types of
            information?
            A.   Store location
            B.   Store logo
            C.   Sponsor name
            D.   Credit card logo
            E.   All of the above

D   7-41.   Cropped artwork can create:
            A.   Action
            B.   A feeling of speed
            C.   Greater attention-getting value
            D.   Two of the above
            E.   All of the above

B 7-42. Which of the following is not a major point in favor of using a photograph
in an advertisement?
A. Impact
B. Fantasy
C. Believability
D. Realism
E. All of the above

A 7-43. When the feeling of fantasy is desirable, all of the following types of
artwork can be effective except:
A. Photograph
B. Diagram
C. Line drawing
D. Cartoon
E. All the above are effective

E 7-44. The use of cartoon artwork in an advertisement:
A. Does not have to be funny
B. Can promote contrast
C. Is somewhat unusual in most media
D. Can promote readership for a product
E. All or none of the above

D 7-45. Which of the following is not a reason for using a line drawing instead of
a photograph in an advertisement?
A. Drawings reveal less information to competitors
B. Drawings print well
C. Drawings are unique and can, therefore, be differentiated
D. Drawings sell more products
E. Drawings can be used in brochures, ads, correspondence, etc.

E 7-46. Which of the following art techniques should not be used to illustrate
reasons for product purchase?
A. Charts
B. Diagrams
C. Graphs
D. Picturegrams
E. None of the above

C 7-47. An advertiser in the United States who seeks to convey a fiery, passionate,
exciting feeling about the product would most likely use what color in the
firm's advertisements:
A. Purple
B. Orange
C. Red
D. Yellow
E. Green

E 7-48. The use of color in an advertisement is not normally:
A. Expensive
B. Affected by whether it is presented in color or color/black and white
C. Significant in presenting an ad message
D. A communicator
E. None of the above

B 7-49. Which of the following is not a primary color?
   A. Yellow
   B. Green
   C. Blue
   D. Red
   E. All of the above are primary colors

D 7-50. What is changed when black or white is added to a basic color?
   A. Chroma
   B. Hue
   C. Tone
   D. Value
   E. None of the above

Completion

7-51. (*Formal*) balance tends to give a feeling of dignity, dependability, and security to an advertisement.

7-52. In television advertising a (*storyboard*) layout is developed that shows action frames as well as copy.

7-53. A/an (*dummy*) is a mock-up of a point of purchase display.

7-54. The optical center is determined as the point which is equidistant from each side of the ad and (*two-thirds*) of the distance from the bottom of the ad.

7-55. The goals of (*movement*) are to get the person to stay with the ad once they have seen it and to see all parts of the ad.

7-56. An ad layout that directs the customers in an obvious or structured manner uses (*direct motion*) to "force" the customers to follow through the entire ad.

7-57. Layout principles include balance, (*movement*), (*proportion*), (*contrast*), (*unity*), and (*personality*).

7-58. The two types of artwork are (*photographs*) and (*drawings*).

7-59. The secondary colors are (*green*), (*orange*), and (*violet*).

7-60. The primary colors are (*yellow*), (*red*), and (*blue*).

CHAPTER 8 - ADVERTISING PRODUCTION

True or False

F 8-1. Advertising production can be divided into two basic parts: print and telecast.

F 8-2. Letterpress is becoming the most popular method of printing in terms of advertising.

F   8-3.   All lithographic printing is offset printing. The reverse is not true.

T   8-4.   Direct lithography is often used to print outdoor ads and other large stock jobs where strong colors are desired.

T   8-5.   The gravure printing method is not in great demand because of the cost of plate preparation.

F   8-6.   While gravure printing requires a recessed surface, lithography and letterpress print from a flat surface.

T   8-7.   The screens used in the serigraphy method of printing are made from metal or fabric.

T   8-8.   A photographically produced stencil permits some shading of colors when the the serigraphy method of printing is used.

F   8-9.   A typeface must convey a personality characteristic in order to be effective in an advertisement.

T   8-10.   The use of too much style and size variety in type is not only confusing but it is also displeasing to the eye.

F   8-11.   Cursive script type looks like handwriting that appears to be connected while in pure script type the letters do not appear to be connected.

T   8-12.   Type may be set by hand for many special purpose jobs such as when ornamental type is used.

T   8-13.   Advertisers can now use computer equipment to create an ad in a form that is suitable for reproduction.

F   8-14.   "Hot" type setting provides an advertiser with instant flexibility.

T   8-15.   Three lines of 24-point type will require one inch of vertical ad space.

F   8-16.   The point system of type measurement does not insure that a line of type will not overlap with the line above or below it.

F   8-17.   While points are basically a horizontal measure, picas are a vertical measure of type.

F   8-18.   Picas and ems give the same horizontal measurement only when 15-point type is in use.

F   8-19.   There are 12 agates to an inch.

T   8-20.   Leads, which are measured in points, are used to put extra spacing between lines of type.

T   8-21.   No leads are used when the type is set solid.

F   8-22.   Quads provide vertical spacing, just as leads provide horizontal spacing in an ad.

T 8-23. A type series includes the different type sizes for a particular typeface.

T 8-24. A font is one size of type in a type series.

T 8-25. Photoengraving can be used for reproducing artwork as well as for type.

F 8-26. A line engraving is more popular than a halftone engraving with advertisers because it provides for various shades of color (tone variation) in an ad.

T 8-27. When using a halftone engraving, good quality paper and a high screen number means good quality reproduction.

F 8-28. Though expensive to create, live television commercials have become the most popular production method for national advertisers.

F 8-29. A live-action ad is another name for a live ad.

T 8-30. A live-action ad may be live, on tape, or on film.

Multiple Choice

C 8-31. The basic methods of printing do not include:
A. Gravure
B. Serigraphy
C. Typography
D. Letterpress
E. All of the above are basic methods of printing

B 8-32. Which of the following statements concerning letterpress printing is false?
A. Its importance in advertising is diminishing.
B. It involves printing from a flat surface.
C. Some people feel that it gives the best overall printing quality, excluding newsprint.
D. It is being replaced by lithography in newspapers and magazines.
E. None of the above

E 8-33. The lithography printing method is becoming popular because of:
A. Its lower cost
B. Its potential to give a high quality impression
C. Its offset capability
D. Two of the above
E. All of the above

D 8-34. Optical effects that can be used in television production include:
    I. Fade   IV. Freeze
   II. Wipe   V. Dissolve
  III. Pump   VI. Dial

A. I, II, III, IV, V
B. I, II, IV, V, VI
C. I, III, IV, V, VI
D. I, II, IV, V
E. I, II, III, IV, V, VI

A   8-35.   Gravure printing is used for magazines which are printed on newsprint
            because:
            A. It is ideal for big production runs where color is used on low-grade
                paper
            B. It uses offset printing so there is no need to reverse the image
            C. It is inexpensive
            D. Both A and C
            E. All of the above

E   8-36.   Which of the following major typefaces conveys a dignified personality
            characteristic?
            A. Old World #2
            B. Xanadu Perfect
            C. American Standard
            D. Bennett Bold
            E. None of the above

E   8-37.   Which of these factors would not be considered by an advertiser when he/she
            selects type for an ad?
            A. Variety
            B. Both A and C
            C. Legibility
            D. Appropriateness
            E. All or none of the above

D   8-38.   Roman type is not characterized by:
            A. Its variation in thickness of various parts of each letter
            B. Its legibility
            C. Its use of serifs
            D. Its modern image
            E. Its variety and contrast

D   8-39.   Block type is:
            A. Characterized by its uniform thickness within each letter
            B. Popular but is less easy to read than script type
            C. Characterized by an absence of serifs or has square serifs
            D. Two of the above
            E. All of the above

A   8-40.   Television production techniques include:
            A. Animation
            B. Videotape
            C. Film
            D. Live
            E. All of the above

C   8-41.   The number of points that equals one inch is:
            A. Thirty-six points
            B. Forty-eight points
            C. Seventy-two points
            D. Eighty points
            E. None of the above

A   8-42.   The number of picas that equal one inch is:
          A.   Six picas
          B.   Twelve picas
          C.   Eighteen picas
          D.   Thirty-six picas
          E.   None of the above

C   8-43.   The number of points in one pica is:
          A.   Four points
          B.   Six points
          C.   Twelve points
          D.   Eighteen points
          E.   None of the above

B   8-44.   Which equation would an advertiser use to determine the number of picas
          needed in a line of type if the point system is used as the horizontal
          measure?
          A.   Horizontal type size x number of ems = total points ÷ points in a pica
          B.   Number of ems x vertical type size = total points ÷ number of points
               in one pica
          C.   Number of points x vertical type size = total points ÷ points
          D.   Vertical type size x number of ems = total points ÷ 15 points
          E.   None of the above

A   8-45.   How much would a newspaper with an agate line rate of $1.50 charge for a
          2 column - 3 inch ad?
          A. $126.00
          B. $96.00
          C. $84.00
          D. $70.00
          E.   None of the above

B   8-46.   Which of the following statements concerning quads is false?
          A.   Quads improve the attention-getting value of an ad.
          B.   Quads provide vertical spacing in the ad.
          C.   Quads are measured in ems or picas.
          D.   Quads improve the readability of the ad.
          E.   All the above are true.

D   8-47.   A typographer needing to determine if a body of type will fit in the space
          provided for an ad may use:
          A.   A type series chart
          B.   The square-inch method
          C.   A type chart showing characters per pica for different fonts of typefaces
          D.   Two of the above
          E.   All of the above

E   8-48.   An advertiser can obtain the necessary artwork for an ad by:
          A.   Commissioning it from an advertising agency
          B.   Buying or leasing it from a photo supply house
          C.   Creating it himself
          D.   Using stock art
          E.   All of the above

104

B   8-49.   <u>Square-Inch Method</u>
                    <u>Point sizes:</u>   <u>Words per square inch:</u>
                         6   50
                         6 on 8   35
                         8   25
                         8 on 10   15

Using the information provided in the chart, determine the amount of layout
space needed for an ad having 525 words of copy set in 6-point type with a
2-point lead.
A.   10.5 square inches
B.   15 square inches
C.   21 square inches
D.   35 square inches
E.   None of the above

B   8-50. If a national advertiser wishes to duplicate its ad for use in local
letterpress media, the local media would require the national ad in what
form:
A.   Velox
B.   Matrix
C.   Slick
D.   Two of the above
E.   All of the above

Completion

8-51. (*Letterpress*) printing is a technique that reproduces an image by means
of placing ink on a raised surface.

8-52. (*Lithography*), commonly called planographic printing, involves printing
from a flat surface with the ink remaining only where the impression is
on the plate.

8-53. Printing from a recessed surface, called (*gravure*) or (*intaglio*) printing,
has the potential of giving a high quality impression.

8-54. (*Typography*) is defined as the style, arrangement, or appearance of typeset
matter.

8-55. When selecting type, an advertiser should consider the following:
(*legibility*), (*appropriateness*), and (*variety*).

8-56. The four major categories of type design are classified as (*block*), (*script*),
(*roman*), and (*ornamental*).

8-57. Small lines that cross the ends of the main parts of each letter of type
are called (*serifs*).

8-58. A copy of a television ad that is made by making a film of the action from
the video screen is know as a/an (*kinescope*).

8-59. A/an (*em*) is the amount of space needed to print the widest letter in the
type size being used.

8-60. The basic production methods in television are (_film_), (_videotape_), and (_live_), while in radio they are (_live_) or (_tape_).

CHAPTER 9 – MEDIA: AN OVERVIEW

True or False

T 9-1. A car with a realtor's sign on it is one example of advertising.

F 9-2. The list of possible media that an advertiser can use is almost endless. Newspaper and radio should appear on every advertiser's list since such media are always found in the media mix.

F 9-3. As a general rule, if the advertiser likes the media, then its use should promote success for the advertiser's product.

T 9-4. The complexity of a product/service/idea as it relates to the target market should be considered in the media selection process.

F 9-5. Message and media decisions can be made without knowledge of the advertising objectives.

F 9-6. The out-of-pocket cost of a newspaper ad costing $1,500 that is seen by 10,000 people is $150.

T 9-7. In calculating the cost-per-person for a commercial, the intelligent advertiser uses the number of target market members as opposed to the total audience.

T 9-8. One goal of most advertisers is to reach the greatest majority of the target market at the lowest possible cost.

F 9-9. An advertiser should always use the media mix that is being used by competitors.

F 9-10. The primary media selectivity determinant for most magazines is geographic coverage.

T 9-11. Some media stress selectivity on the basis of more than one variable.

F 9-12. In advertising, coverage is only important to television and radio stations.

T 9-13. If is usually difficult to determine the coverage/circulation of a particular advertising vehicle in a small market area.

T 9-14. Though knowledge of a media's circulation figures is important, an advertiser should be more interested in knowing what portion of his target market is found in those figures.

T 9-15. An advertiser should expect to pay more for a particular space or time for the ad to be run as compared to a ROP or ROS buy.

F 9-16. The timing or spacing of a particular advertisement is seldom crucial to the success of the advertising campaign.

F   9-17.   Circulation is defined as the availability of a particular media in the market.

F   9-18.   The advertiser is not required to abide by the restrictions of the media he is using.

T   9-19.   Learning about media restrictions early allows the advertiser to meet the requirements with minimum delay and cost and/or search for different media.

T   9-20.   Though media flexibility is useful at times, it may encourage advertisers to create an advertisement to meet the competition without giving the ad much thought.

F   9-21.   A national manufacturer of men's suits would most likely feel that flexibility was the most important factor in choosing its advertising media.

F   9-22.   Permanence in an advertisement is always desirable.

T   9-23.   Permanence can be obtained in the broadcast media through repetition by means of slogans or jingles.

F   9-24.   Customer acceptance of a particular media will not have an impact on the effectiveness of an advertisement in that media.

F   9-25.   An advertiser can expect to get the same quality production when using the same screen size for a newspaper ad and for a magazine ad.

T   9-26.   An advertiser should note the differences in the quality of workmanship of each media firm.

T   9-27.   The key to specialty advertising support for an ad message is its usefulness to the market.

T   9-28.   The editorial content of a newspaper on any given day may be detrimental to some ads and supportive of others.

T   9-29.   Potential benefits may develop over a period of time from a long-term media arrangement.

F   9-30.   It pays for an advertiser to cultivate a long-term relationship with a particular media even if the other criteria of media selection are not met.

Multiple Choice

E   9-31.   Which of the following are types of media?

       I.   Theater   IV.   Direct mail
      II.   Transit   V.   Skywriting
     III.   Flyer   VI.   Directory

       A.   I, II, IV, V
       B.   II, III, IV, V
       C.   I, III, IV, VI
       D.   III, IV, V, VI
       E.   All of the above

C 9-32. If the advertiser knows his target market consists of white male doctors, age 25-40, earning $35,000 or more, he is most likely to choose which of the following as his/her media choice?
A. Television prime time
B. Cosmopolitan
C. American Medical Association Journal
D. Newspaper
E. All of the above

A 9-33. A duplicating machine manufacturer would most likely select which of the following media choices as a means of promoting its products?
A. Business magazine
B. Radio
C. Newspaper
D. Specialty
E. Point of purchase

D 9-34. The CPM figure for a $160,000 television commercial that was seen by an audience of 4 million people is:
A. .004
B. .04
C. 4
D. 40
E. None of the above

A 9-35. Which of the following statements concerning media selectivity is false?
A. Movie magazines are read by teenagers and the white collar market.
B. Radio stations in a town typically appeal to different market groups.
C. Magazines offer selectivity on the basis of life-style and demographics.
D. Newspapers are primarily a geographic medium.
E. None of the above.

E 9-36. Which of the following are factors to consider when comparing the various media?
    I. Quality of workmanship   IV. Media flexibility
    II. Product characteristics   V. Media life
    III. Media support   VI. Advertising objectives

A. II, III, IV, VI
B. I, II, V, VI
C. II, III, IV, V
D. I, II, III, IV
E. All of the above

D 9-37. The penetration figure for an advertisement that is broadcast on a television station with a coverage of 2,700,000 people is:
A. 1,200,000
B. 1,350,000
C. 2,700,000
D. More information is needed
E. None of the above

E   9-38. When discussing a particular media's coverage, an advertiser should:
          A. Determine the portion of his market found in that figure
          B. Be wary of the use of the interchangeable terms: circulation and coverage
          C. Ask how circulation data were determined
          D. Both B and C
          E. All of the above

B   9-39. A limitation of firms such as Nielsen and Arbitron is that their data:
          A. Are useless to advertisers
          B. Are available primarily for the national media and large market centers
          C. Are not updated very frequently
          D. Must be funded by the individual advertiser
          E. All of the above

C   9-40. Advertisers can obtain information from national services such as Nielsen on:
          A. A particular media's coverage in any size market
          B. The penetration figure for local media
          C. The number of people who view media which carry advertising
          D. Both A and C
          E. All of the above

E   9-41. Media availability refers to:
          A. Time availability of media
          B. Availability of desired media
          C. Space availability of media
          D. Both A and C
          E. All of the above

D   9-42. Time and space availability depends on:
          A   The practices of the particular media
          B. The other advertisers in the area
          C. The practice of selling advertisements on a run-of-station or
              run-of-paper basis
          D. Both A and B
          E. All of the above

E   9-43. Which of the following would not be a media restriction for an advertiser?
          A. The mailing weight restrictions imposed by the U.S. Post Office
          B. The number of pages allocated to a single advertiser by the media
          C. The halftone screen size restrictions of Newsweek magazine
          D. The Television Code's restrictions on the types of ads that can be run
              on television
          E. All of the above are media restrictions

B   9-44. The media which are best known for their advertising flexibility are:
          A. Newspapers and direct mail
          B. Radio and newspapers
          C. Television and radio
          D. Magazines and direct mail
          E. Advertising specialties and magazines

B 9-45. An advertiser seeking permanence for his ad would choose a:
A. Radio jingle
B. Magazine
C. Daily newspaper
D. Television
E. Sunday newspaper

A 9-46. The media life of a Sunday newspaper is generally:
A. Several days
B. One week
C. 24 hours
D. 1 hour
E. None of the above

C 9-47. Which of the following statements concerning media acceptance is false?
A. A trade ad should be in the media that is read by the majority of persons involved in that industry.
B. An ad run in an acceptable media may carry more clout than an ad in a different media vehicle.
C. An advertiser should select the media that he thinks an ad should be run in for both the consumer and trade markets.
D. Image is a factor in media acceptance.
E. All the above are true.

A 9-48. An advertiser seeking a good quality print advertisement that will reach a carefully selected demographic market would choose to advertise in a:
A. Magazine
B. Newspaper
C. Newspaper rotogravure supplement
D. Two of the above
E. All of the above

C 9-49. All of the following media typically lack editorial support except:
A. Outdoor advertising
B. Point-of-purchase advertising
C. Radio advertising
D. Direct mail advertising
E. None of the above

D 9-50. In terms of broadcast advertising, which is the more important figure - coverage, circulation, or penetration?
A. Coverage
B. Circulation
C. Penetration
D. B and C are the same and are more important
E. A and C are the same and are more important

Completion

9-51. Advertising cost may be viewed in two ways: (*out-of-pocket cost*) and (*cost-per-person*).

9-52. Assume that an ad that cost $10,000 was read by 200,000 people. The CPM figure for this ad is (*50*).

110

9-53. The number of potential viewers/readers/listeners for an advertisement is shown by the circulation or (_penetration_) figure for that particular medium.

9-54. In terms of media selectivity, two types of selectivity are common: (_geographic_) and (_demographic_).

9-55. If a radio station reaches an area containing 500,000 people, then the 500,000 figure is known as that station's (_coverage_) figure.

9-56. Media availability is a two-step question. Is the (_desired media_) available? If yes, then is the (_desired time or space_) available?

9-57. A talk show's use of an integrated commercial is an example of media (_support_).

9-58. Nonadvertising customer information - news, features, etc. - provided by the medium whose purpose is to draw attention to the medium is known as (_editorial support_).

9-59. Without knowledge of the (_target market_), or who will buy the product, it is very difficult to select the appropriate media for use in an advertising campaign.

9-60. There are at least fifteen factors that should be kept in mind whenever the question of media selection is under review. These fifteen factors are: (_target market_), (_product characteristics_), (_advertising objectives_), (_cost_), (_competitor advertising_), (_media selectivity_), (_media coverage_), (_media availability_), (_media restrictions_), (_media flexibility_), (_media life_), (_media acceptance_), (_quality of workmanship_), (_media support_), and (_media benefits_).

CHAPTER 10 - PUBLICATION MEDIA

True or False

F 10-1. Magazines are the most popular advertising media in terms of dollars spent on advertising.

F 10-2. All tabloid newspapers today are 10 x 14 inches in size.

F 10-3. A newspaper's page size is directly related to the number of columns on the page.

T 10-4. A magazine can raise or lower advertising rates in two ways: change the line rate or alter the guaranteed circulation base.

T 10-5. Though they follow the news format, papers that come out on an "as-needed" basis are not "news" papers.

T 10-6. Specialized newspapers such as The Wall Street Journal concentrate on a particular subject, though they may also carry general news.

T 10-7. The advertiser should select a newspaper or magazine whose market audience matches the target market for the firm's product/service/idea.

F   10-8.   Newspapers are considered to be local media.

T   10-9.   Retailers favor the use of newspapers for their advertising needs since newspapers generally serve a well-defined geographic area.

T   10-10. For newspapers, flexibility can possibly be achieved in terms of the area served and thereby waste little circulation.

T   10-11. For newspapers and magazines, editorial support can be improved upon with proper advertising placement.

T   10-12. The lack of permanence for a newspaper ad can be viewed as both a positive and a negative attribute of the medium.

F   10-13. Newspapers generally concentrate on the demographics of the market to be served.

T   10-14. Some specialized newspapers consider certain demographic variables in their editorial copy as well as in their advertising.

F   10-15. A true island position in newspaper advertising is quite common.

T   10-16. A newspaper that does not have a special rate structure for particular ad placements is free to place all ads where it wishes to place them.

F   10-17. Evening newspapers normally cover a larger geographic area in terms of the audience or number of readers than morning papers.

T   10-18. The ABC Audit Report gives a newspaper's circulation performance, defines the market the paper serves, and gives the media buyer an indication of how well the paper covers its market.

F   10-19. The national newspaper advertising rate is almost always cheaper than the local rate even before discounts are considered.

F   10-20. There is a standard combination arrangement among newspapers that is set up by the Standard Rate and Data Service. This helps to simplify the job of media buyers.

T   10-21. The "local" newspaper is the better buy in most cases, when compared to a larger metropolitan newspaper on an adjusted milline rate basis.

F   10-22. A Hi-Fi preprint has a fixed cutoff point while a Spectracolor preprint has a repeated pattern like wallpaper so it doesn't matter where the newsprint is cut.

T   10-23. Retailers are the dominant users of newspaper advertising at the local level.

T   10-24. The trend toward the flat magazine size could mean ad layout standardization for the advertiser at some time in the future.

F   10-25. The majority of magazines are issued bimonthly.

T   10-26. Farm magazines reflect climate and crop differences by being a geographic medium as well as a demographic medium.

F   10-27.   Due to the flexibility of magazines, an advertiser can usually make last minute ad changes in a manner that is similar to newspapers.

T   10-28.   If the area served is small, the cost of ad placement and ad production makes the magazine ad expensive on a relative basis.

T   10-29.   Magazine advertisers use the ABC Report to determine reader acceptability by studying the data which shows the amount of new and renewal subscriptions.

F   10-30.   An advertiser must pay a fixed amount for every magazine sold in excess of the guaranteed circulation amount, while a refund is received if the base circulation figure is not met.

Multiple Choice

D   10-31.   The most popular media form available to the advertiser is the publication media which include:
A.   Newspapers
B.   Brochures
C.   Magazines
D.   Two of the above
E.   All of the above

B   10-32.   The various kinds of newspapers and magazines are classified by all the following except:
A.   Content
B.   Advertisements
C.   Size/format
D.   Market audience
E.   None of the above

A   10-33.   The goal of the American Newspaper Publishers Association is to reduce the number of ad formats in use from 214 to:
A.   Six
B.   Twenty
C.   Fifty
D.   Ninety
E.   None of the above

C   10-34.   Papers that are published on an "as-needed" basis are used predominately to:
A.   Give the news
B.   Update local gossip
C.   Inform special groups of coming attractions and events
D.   Both A and C
E.   All of the above

C   10-35.   In terms of advertising, all the following are generally advantages of newspapers except:
A.   Editorial support
B.   Geographic selectivity
C.   Quality of product
D.   Flexibility
E.   None of the above

B   10-36. Which statement concerning newspaper editorial support is false?
         A. Ad placements improve on the editorial support of a paper.
         B. A sporting goods ad is normally not helped by being placed on the
             sports page.
         C. The newspaper lends support to the advertising on its pages.
         D. Editorial content may sometimes be detrimental to the ad.
         E. None of the above

E   10-37. The disadvantages of newspaper advertising typically include:
         A. Poor quality of product
         B. Lack of permanence
         C. Limited demographic orientation
         D. Poor environment for ad placement
         E. All of the above

E   10-38. The term "preferred position" refers to:
         A. An ad placed on the last page of a newspaper section
         B. Ad placement in the sports section for a sporting goods ad.
         C. An island or full position on a particular page
         D. Ad placement "above the fold" on the page
         E. All of the above

A   10-39. In newspaper advertising, full position refers to an ad placed:
         A. In the upper right corner of the page
         B. Following editorial copy
         C. Next to editorial copy
         D. All of the above
         E. None of the above

A   10-40. The Audit Bureau of Circulations provides the newspaper advertiser with all
             the following except:
         A. Subscription rates
         B. Audience measurements
         C. Independent circulation figures
         D. Demographic data
         E. All of the above are provided

B   10-41. The local rate for newspaper advertising is all the following except:
         A. Low in cost
         B. Quoted in agate lines
         C. Subject to volume discounts
         D. Not subject to agency commissions
         E. Usually restricted to advertisers selling to the ultimate consumer

A   10-42. The national rate for newspaper advertising is not:
         A. Subject to a volume discount
         B. Quoted in agate lines
         C. More expensive than the local rate
         D. Subject to agency commissions
         E. All of the above are true

114

C   10-43. A general cost estimate for a full-color preprint for a newspaper ad is
             in the area of:
             A. 10 to 15 percent above the full-color ROP ad rate
             B. 25 to 50 percent above the full-color ROP ad rate
             C. 50 to 75 percent above the full-color ROP ad rate
             D. 75 to 100 percent above the full-color ROP ad rate
             E. 100 to 150 percent above the full-color ROP ad rate

D   10-44. Many newspaper advertisers have replaced direct distribution and direct
             mail advertising with the use of:
             A. Display advertising
             B. Sunday magazine supplements
             C. Classified ads
             D. Tabloid inserts
             E. All of the above

C   10-45. Which of the following is not a common magazine size today?
             A. Flat
             B. Standard
             C. Tabloid
             D. Pocket
             E. Large

B   10-46. Which of the following classes is not a category when magazines are
             classified in terms of content and market?
             A. Farm market
             B. International market
             C. Business market
             D. Consumer market
             E. None of the above

D   10-47. A major disadvantage of advertising in a magazine is:
             A. Quality of workmanship
             B. Demographic selectivity
             C. Editorial support
             D. Limited availability
             E. Permanence

A   10-48. The limited availability of a magazine refers to all of the following except:
             A. Some magazines restrict the amount of money a particular advertiser may
                 spend per issue
             B. Various magazines restrict what can be advertised in their pages
             C. Most magazines do not serve small local markets
             D. Some magazines restrict the size of the ads
             E. None of the above

C   10-49. Which of the following is not a preferred position for a magazine ad?
             A. Next to the table of contents
             B. The center
             C. Toward the back of the magazine
             D. Inside front cover
             E. Flexform positioning

D   10-50.   A magazine can raise/lower its advertising rates by:
            A.   Changing the dual rate
            B.   Changing the line rate
            C.   Altering the guaranteed circulation base
            D.   Two of the above
            E.   All of the above

Completion

10-51.   A newspaper that comes out (*four*) or more times a week is considered
          a daily newspaper.

10-52.   A (*preferred position*) in newspaper advertising is any position that is
          situated in such a way as to promote the attention-getting qualities of
          the ad or that is next to editorial copy.

10-53.   In newspaper advertising, the (*full*) position, next to and following
          editorial copy, is desirable since it benefits from editorial support.

10-54.   The most desirable ad placement position in a newspaper is the (*island*)
          position which has editorial support on at least three sides of the ads.

10-55.   If a newspaper with a circulation of 500,000 readers has a line rate of $5,
          then the milline rate for that paper is (*10*).

10-56.   When a morning and evening paper in an area are owned by the same firm,
          an advertiser may be offered a (*combination*) rate, which is more expensive
          than one paper but less than if both papers were purchased separately.

10-57.   The adjusted milline rate formula uses the (*target market*) circulation
          figure instead of the total circulation so that newspapers can be compared
          without the waste circulation factor.

10-58.   In recent years the trend in magazine size has moved to the (*flat*)
          magazine size.

10-59.   A magazine advertiser whose ad is surrounded by editorial copy on the page
          is using the advertising form known as (*flexform*) which is considered
          a preferred position.

10-60.   A (*bleed*) ad is one where the printing or color goes to the edge of the
          page instead of being limited to the area within the publication's
          margins.

CHAPTER 11 - BROADCAST MEDIA

True or False

T   11-1.   Broadcast media are important to advertisers since so many homes have both
              television and radio sets and they use them.

F   11-2.   Man-made and natural barriers have little or no effect on the signal pattern
              for a FM broadcast station. The opposite is true for the signal pattern of
              an AM broadcast station.

T   11-3.   Many local and regional AM stations are limited to daytime operation by the Federal Communications Commission, the broadcast media regulatory body.

F   11-4.   A major advantage of FM stereo multiplex radio stations is that they put out a stronger signal than regular FM stations, everything else being equal.

T   11-5.   While some radio stations choose a program format that serves one target market, many small town stations may serve all markets by changing the program format throughout the day.

F   11-6.   The Pulse, Inc. uses the diary method, whereas Arbitron uses the interview technique to determine who listens to radio.

T   11-7.   Since radio is primarily a local media, it may be the cheapest form of advertising per ad for most advertisers.

T   11-8.   A lack of visual support is not always a problem in radio advertising since you can create a "picture" with words and sounds.

F   11-9.   Radio is primarily a nighttime medium in terms of customer listening patterns.

T   11-10. Preferred radio advertising times are somewhat dependent on the particular shows to be carried by the station.

F   11-11. On the average, radio reaches 95.4 percent of the U. S. population each day.

T   11-12. An advertiser or radio station can have almost any type of audience information that would be of interest for a fee.

F   11-13. In terms of audience measurement, the frequency of impressions made on one person is irrelevant in a GRP calculation.

T   11-14. Due to the competition among stations, an advertiser may find that radio rates are usually subject to negotiation.

F   11-15. Of all television households, 98 percent can receive ultra high frequency (UHF) signals.

T   11-16. Television programming can originate with the local station or with the network.

F   11-17. An advertiser uses ADI data to determine the penetration level of the organization's television ads.

T   11-18. The Area of Dominant Influence is a geographic market design that defines one television market to the exclusion of another by means of measurable viewing patterns.

F   11-19. The demonstration commercial is television's least effective advertising format.

T   11-20. It may be cheaper for an advertiser to show his product in several magazine ads than in one television ad.

F 11-21. The National Association of Broadcasters Code permits 10 consecutive television commercials to be run on a participating code station.

T 11-22. The number of ads on television reduces the effectiveness of the ads carried by the medium.

F 11-23. Television ads run in the middle of a string of consecutive ads have the lowest recall scores of all ads in the ad series.

T 11-24. Television ads aired during prime time hours normally carry a premium rate.

F 11-25. As far as the advertiser is concerned, preferred times are a function of the network or the station, rather than the target market.

F 11-26. An Audimeter is used to determine who watches television.

F 11-27. A coincidental telephone survey can be taken at any time to determine who watches a particular program by age and sex.

T 11-28. The coincidental telephone survey is important to broadcaster and advertiser since it provides almost instant information on television viewer patterns.

T 11-29. An advertiser who wants to insure that his television ad will be run may pay double the amount the advertiser will pay who buys a preemptive ad.

F 11-30. Participation sponsorship is gaining in popularity in television advertising but it is still not as popular as program sponsorship.

Multiple Choice

B 11-31. If a radio ad is heard by 25 percent of the population at least two times, the number of GRP's for that particular ad is:
A. 25
B. 50
C. 75
D. 100
E. None of the above

C 11-32. Which, if any, of the following is not a type of AM radio station?
A. "Local"
B. "Clear" channel
C. "National"
D. "Regional"
E. None of the above

D 11-33. Frequency modulation stations are classified by:
A. Stereo or nonstereo
B. Power output and antenna height
C. "Clear" channel
D. Two of the above
E. All of the above

A   11-34. A disadvantage of using radio for your advertising needs is a lack of:
            A. Visual support
            B. Geographic/demographic selectivity
            C. Low out-of-pocket expenses
            D. Flexibility
            E. None of the above

C   11-35. Demographic selectivity is usually present in a multi-station radio market
            since the various stations serve:
            A. The markets by time of day
            B. An area of 10-25 miles
            C. Different markets within the coverage area
            D. Two of the above
            E. All of the above

B   11-36. A radio ad, unlike print media or television, must really "work" to get
            the attention of the target audience because radio is:
            A. A geographic medium
            B. A background medium
            C. Expensive
            D. Flexible
            E. None of the above

D   11-37. The preferred time for most radio advertising is:
            A. Sunday morning worship time
            B. Talk show time
            C. Soap opera time
            D. Commuting drive time
            E. All of the above

E   11-38. From 1968 to 1980, the size of the total radio audience grew by:
            A. 2 percent
            B. 5 percent
            C. 13 percent
            D. 16 percent
            E. None of the above

A   11-39. An advertiser buying air time on a UHF television station needs to be aware
            of all the following problems except:
            A. Many television sets today don't receive the UHF signal
            B. The audience size may be limited by the signal quality
            C. UHF television signal transmissions are hampered by tall building and
                other structures
            D. Two of the above
            E. All of the above

C   11-40. Cable television started in 1950 as a means of:
            A. Bringing outside stations to the viewer
            B. Originating some programming
            C. Bringing t.v. to those unable to receive a television signal due to
                distance or terrain
            D. Directly communicating with the viewer
            E. All of the above

E   11-41. Subscription television:
               A. May use cable station lines to carry its signal
               B. Alters the effectiveness of commercial television advertising
               C. Is typified by Home Box Office
               D. Offers the viewer an alternative to watching commercial television
               E. All of the above are correct

B   11-42. Which of the following is not a type of televison signal?
               A. VHF
               B. Local
               C. UHF
               D. Cable
               E. None of the above

B   11-43. Which of the following is not an advantage of television?
               A. Geographic selectivity
               B. Flexibility
               C. Show and tell
               D. Penetration
               E. None of the above

A   11-44. The disadvantages of television as an advertising medium do not include:
               A. Background medium
               B. Cost
               C. Clutter
               D. Perishability
               E. None of the above

D   11-45. Which statement concerning the perishability of television is false?
               A. Ad repetition improves the life of the ad
               B. Due to the cost, ad repetition is more difficult
               C. An ad is gone once it is aired unless the receiver is a video-recorder
               D. Ad perishability is viewed as an advantage for television
               E. None of the above

A   11-46. The highest recall score in a string of five consecutive television
             commercials is usually found to be the ad in the:
               A. First position
               B. Second position
               C. Third position
               D. Fourth position
               E. Fifth position

E   11-47. Broadcast audience measurement data on the national level is determined
             from:
               A. Overnight surveys
               B. Diaries
               C. Meters
               D. Both A and C
               E. All of the above

120

D   11-48. A problem with the diary technique which is used to study television
            viewer patterns is that:
            A. A diary isn't provided for every T.V. set in the house
            B. The diary can be used to collect data on the viewer
            C. The viewer forgets the diary
            D. The viewer writes down what he thinks he should have watched instead
                what was watched
            E. None of the above

B   11-49. Nielsen does not use its Audimeter to:
            A. Determine what television station the set is tuned to
            B. Determine who views the television set
            C. Determine when a television set is on
            D. Provide an objective measure of the activity of a T.V. set 24 hours
                a day
            E. None of the above

E   11-50. Of all television ad lengths, the most popular is the:
            A. 10 second spot
            B. 20 second spot
            C. 30 second spot
            D. 60 second spot
            E. Two of the above

Completion

11-51. (*Clear channel*) AM radio stations are on a channel all to themselves during
        nighttime hours and can transmit a signal up to 700 miles.

11-52. The FCC regulates the (*power output*) and the (*antenna height*) for FM radio
        stations as a means of controlling signal distance.

11-53. Though radio ads do lack permanence, (*repetition*) of the ad does reduce
        perishability.

11-54. Since many broadcast ads are presented in a short period of time, the
        resulting (*clutter*) makes it difficult for any particular ad to stand out
        from the others.

11-55. Average (*quarter hour*) ratings give the percent of the population listening
        to a station during an average quarter hour in a given time period. (*CUME*)
        ratings indicate the percentage listening at least once during the time
        period.

11-56. The (*Gross Rating Point*) calculation for a radio ad determines the level of
        advertising impact by considering both ad reach and frequency.

11-57. The three categories of radio advertising use are: (*network*), (*spot*), and
        (*local*).

11-58. Local television programming mainly consists of (*syndicated*) shows which
        are features that are purchased/leased by a station to be shown over that
        station.

11-59. The (*Area of Dominant Influence*) is a geographic market design that defines each television market exclusive of another based on measurable viewing patterns.

11-60. A station break ad that is viewed between shows, which is called (*announcement*) sponsorship, allows the television advertiser to advertise without being identified with a show.

CHAPTER 12 - DIRECT MEDIA

True or False

F   12-1. Advertising that asks a prospect to take some type of action now is called action advertising.

T   12-2. By definition, direct mail advertising includes all forms of mailed direct advertising, except mail order.

F   12-3. Direct advertising is made up of two components: direct mail advertising and mail order advertising.

F   12-4. Direct advertising is often called sales promotion.

T   12-5. A person who requests more information or enters an accompanying sweepstakes without purchasing the advertised item is still making a direct response to the direct mail ad.

F   12-6. Mail order advertising offers goods and services to present and potential prospects through various promotional media in order to effect a direct action response by mail, telephone, or personal visit.

F   12-7. Good direct mail advertising letters must be short.

T   12-8. Postcards bearing a personal advertising message must be mailed first class, while those having a standard message may be sent third class.

T   12-9. A bed sheet's, or broadside's, greatest strength is its size.

T   12-10. Since circulars appear to be inexpensive, advertisers should be careful of the image that circulars project for the advertised product.

F   12-11. Permanence, flexibility, and impact are thought to be advantages of direct mail while selectivity, cost, and lack of editorial support are cited as disadvantages.

F   12-12. Direct mail has the advantage of selectivity because there is little to distract the customer from it such as news stories or other ads.

T   12-13. No media is suited better than direct mail/direct response advertising for measuring advertising results.

F   12-14. Direct mail has the advantage of being a low cost-per-person medium.

122

T   12-15. For many, direct mail is synonymous with junk mail. Therefore, a carefully
            selected target market is important for direct mail success.

T   12-16. Since mailing list sources are numerous, a mailing list can be found for
            almost any marketing situation.

F   12-17. Once a good mailing list has been compiled, maintaining it is no problem
            so long as computers are available.

T   12-18. The most productive list available to an advertiser is thought to be the
            house list of customers who have already made purchases.

F   12-19. Compiled mailing lists refer to people who have done something, while rented
            lists refer to people who are something.

T   12-20. Firms that rent out mailing lists may include dummy or seed names in the
            list in order to check to see if the advertiser uses the list again
            without paying again for the names.

T   12-21. An advertiser may increase his rate of return for direct mail by using
            trial offers, sweepstakes, request cards, and other devices and, thereby,
            gain more rental-free names for use in future mailings.

F   12-22. A mailing list which is acquired by exchanging names with another firm
            is the most effective source of direct mail lists.

F   12-23. Younger people (under 25) are better potential direct mail customers than
            those over 25.

T   12-24. A direct mail mailing list that is rented from an appropriate source will
            normally sell better than a compiled list.

F   12-25. The response from a particular mailing list will always vary by region,
            state, zip code, etc. in the manner expected of the product.

F   12-26. The most effective computer letter uses the prospect's name often (at least
            six times) throughout the letter.

T   12-27. Whether a direct mail letter is printed on only one side of the paper or on
            both sides should depend in part on the demographics of the target market.

T   12-28. The costs associated with direct mail include list acquisition, mail piece
            preparation, printing, and postage.

T   12-29. Breakeven analysis is useful in determining if you need to better control
            your mailing list circulation.

F   12-30. Television is the second most popular medium for direct response advertising.

Multiple Choice

B   12-31.   The definition for direct advertising does not encompass the following:
          A.   A selected target market
          B.   A personal sales call
          C.   A controlled circulation
          D.   A written printed, or processed advertising message
          E.   None of the above is incorrect

C   12-32.   Which category of direct media is not a type of direct advertising?
          A.   Mail order advertising
          B.   Unmailed direct advertising
          C.   Direct response advertising
          D.   Direct mail advertising
          E.   None of the above

D   12-33.   Which of the following are major functions of direct mail advertising?
            I.   To close a sale
           II.   To familiarize prospects with distributor names
          III.   To aid customers in buying
           IV.   To arouse interest
            V.   To inform a larger market about your product/service/idea
           VI.   To familiarize prospects with a product's merits

          A.   I, III, IV, VI
          B.   II, III, IV, V
          C.   I, II, III, VI
          D.   II, III, IV, VI
          E.   II, IV, V, VI

D   12-34.   Unmailed direct advertising may be distributed by:
          A.   An in-store counter display
          B.   A mail order catalog left on your doorstep
          C.   A promotional piece delivered to your door
          D.   Two of the above
          E.   All of the above

E   12-35.   Direct marketing encompasses:
          A.   Mail order advertising
          B.   Direct response advertising
          C.   Personal selling
          D.   Two of the above
          E.   All of the above

A   12-36.   Of the following, which are forms of direct mail that are available to an
          advertiser?
            I.   Postcards   IV.   Circulars
           II.   Placards   V.   Stuffers
          III.   Broadsides   VI.   Billboards

          A.   I, III, IV, V
          B.   I, II, IV, V
          C.   II, III, V, VI
          D.   III, IV, V, VI
          E.   I, II, III, V

124

C   12-37. A brochure is not:
             A. The most popular form of "booklet" in use
             B. Used in direct mail advertising
             C. As inexpensive as most circulars
             D. Used in non-mail direct advertising
             E. None of the above are correct

B   12-38. Of the following statements concerning catalog direct mail advertising,
             which is/are false?
             A. Many firms sell exclusively through catalogs.
             B. Sears, Roebuck & Company issued the first catalog in 1872.
             C. Catalogs are designed to be kept as a reference book or a sales tool.
             D. Catalogs are expensive and therefore should only be distributed to
                 prospects.
             E. All statements are false.

B   12-39. All the following are advantages of direct mail except the lack of:
             A. Flexibility
             B. Reader interest
             C. Selectivity
             D. Permanence
             E. Impact

D   12-40. The flexibility of direct mail advertising is restrained by the:
             A. Size of budget
             B. Size of paper
             C. Postal regulations
             D. Two of the above
             E. All of the above

A   12-41. Direct mail has the advantage of impact except possibly in the month of:
             A. January
             B. March
             C. May
             D. August
             E. December

E   12-42. The direct mail advertiser is working to overcome the lack of editorial
             support when he/she makes use of:
             A. Television ads which promote the direct mail piece
             B. Sweepstakes
             C. Free gifts
             D. Two of the above
             E. All of the above

E   12-43. A mailing list for a direct mail advertiser cannot be obtained by:
             A. Exchanging lists with others
             B. Using a professional compiler's services
             C. Compiling it yourself
             D. Obtaining a rented list
             E. All of the above can be used

A   12-44. An advertiser who is compiling his/her own mailing list would be most
            likely to use all of the following sources except:
            A. List brokers
            B. Internal records
            C. Telephone directory
            D. Shipping records
            E. Business directories

D   12-45. All of the following statements concerning rented mailing lists are true
            except:
            A. A list of persons who made a direct response is better than a list
                from a general source.
            B. It is important to know who is currently using the list you want to
                rent.
            C. A list that is closely related to the advertiser's customer is best.
            D. Magazine subscription lists represent a good source for mail order
                customers.
            E. All the above are true.

E   12-46. An advertiser using a rented list would want to know:
            A. How the list is updated
            B. Who else has used the list
            C. When the list was developed
            D. How the list was developed
            E. All of the above

E   12-47. Rural dwellers are better direct mail customers than city dwellers because
            of:
            A. Coincidence
            B. Habit
            C. Convenience
            D. Only B and C
            E. All of the above

D   12-48. A mailing list of customer names compiled in-house will probably draw more
            response than:
            A. A direct response list
            B. A rented list
            C. A professionally compiled list
            D. All of the above
            E. None of the above

C   12-49. All the following statements concerning the mail piece effectiveness of an
            envelope are true except:
            A. A mail piece using a mailing label is usually effective.
            B. An enclosed envelope is more effective than an enclosed card.
            C. A mail piece without a return address is usually effective.
            D. A mail piece in an envelope is more effective than a self-mailer.
            E. Guaranteed postage does not affect the response.

C   12-50. Which of the following statements is true?
            A. All direct advertising is included in direct marketing.
            B. All direct response advertising in included in direct advertising.
            C. All mail order advertising is included in direct response advertising.
            D. All direct marketing is included in direct response advertising.
            E. All statements are true.

Completion

12-51. A (*compiled*) list contains names of people who are something while a (*rented*)
        list contains names of people who have done something.

12-52. The most widely used form of direct media is (*direct mail*) advertising.

12-53. The form of direct media that is responsible for the entire selling job is
        known as (*mail order*) advertising.

12-54. The (*letter*) is the most popular form of direct mail advertising.

12-55. A (*circular*), or throwaway, featuring one or more items is one of the
        lowest cost forms of direct mail advertising.

12-56. As a form of direct mail, (*catalogs*) are the opposite of circulars as
        they are planned as a reference book or a complete sales tool and are more
        expensive than brochures.

12-57. The disadvantages of direct mail advertising are lack of (*reader interest*),
        lack of (*editorial support*), and (*cost*).

12-58. (*Direct marketing*) is a marketing system that offers products and services
        to present and potential customers and prospects through the use of various
        promotional media, singly or in combination, to effect a direct action
        response by mail, telephone, or personal visit.

12-59. The best month for mail order response is (*January*).

12-60. Census data indicate that (*20%*) of the population change their place of
        residence in a given year.

CHAPTER 13 - MOBILE MEDIA

True or False

F   13-1. Transit advertising is the oldest form of advertising as shown by evidence
           that was found by archeologists in the Middle East.

F   13-2. In order to be effective, outdoor advertising requires narrow roads and
           slow speeds.

F   13-3. Roadside signs are classified as a nonstandardized form of outdoor
           advertising because they are poorly constructed and are usually in disrepair.

T   13-4.   An on-premise sign should be reinforced by the other advertising in use so that when the customer sees the sign, she will identify it with the product/service that is advertised.

T   13-5.   An advertising spectacular may make use of 3-dimensional components with flashing lights, and/or an electronic message board. Since it is usually expensive, the spectacular should be placed in a high-traffic location.

F   13-6.   All posters, as a standardized media, fit in one frame size and allow for no variance in the area used for advertising.

F   13-7.   A bulletin, like a spectacular, cannot be moved from one location to another.

T   13-8.   A standardized bulletin has approximately three times as much square footage of advertising space as a poster.

F   13-9.   A highway location with fast moving traffic is the most desirable position for the effective use of a trivision bulletin by an advertiser.

T   13-10.   Outdoor advertising has the potential of reaching all of the population numerous times within its period of use.

T   13-11.   The outdoor medium has a high level of flexibility in terms of market selectivity.

F   13-12.   The cost-per-thousand (CPM) figure for outdoor advertising is high, making it an unattractive media for many advertisers.

T   13-13.   Though the size of a billboard or bulletin alone will not guarantee the advertiser success, it does promote attention-getting effectiveness.

T   13-14.   Since outdoor advertising is a form of mass media, it should not be used by an advertiser trying to promote an exclusive image.

F   13-15.   In making his location choice for outdoor advertising, the advertiser should be concerned about the proximity of other boards, but need not be concerned about structures, buildings, etc.

F   13-16.   The two classifications of outdoor posters are sheet posters and exterior displays. Sheet posters come in either 24 or 30 sheets, while all exterior displays are bleed posters.

F   13-17.   The original AMMO (Phase I) revealed the size of the outdoor showing needed to deliver a desired number of GRP's to a particular demographic group.

T   13-18.   Bulletins are likely to have a high potential reach since most are placed in high traffic locations.

F   13-19.   The basic advertising rate for a poster includes the board rent and the production costs.

T   13-20.   The advertising poster is purchased for a minimum time of one month, while a bulletin is usually purchased for a year or more.

T   13-21. Many outdoor companies have available a rotary plan that calls for moving a bulletin periodically throughout the contract period.

F   13-22. Car cards, exterior displays, and station displays are used exclusively in conjunction with bus travel.

T   13-23. Take-one car cards are one way to use direct response advertising in conjunction with mobile media.

T   13-24. As with car cards, exterior display sizes are standardized, thereby allowing the national advertiser to design and print one size poster to be distributed nationwide for ad placement.

T   13-25. Even though the target market may not be transit users, an advertiser can use transit advertising successfully in a particular geographic area.

F   13-26. An advertiser can obtain impact by purchasing a "total bus" (where all the ads on the interior of the bus are for one company/product).

T   13-27. Transit media are economical when considering the cost-per-potential exposure, thereby making transit advertising very useful as a supportive medium.

F   13-28. The least effective position for an exterior transit ad is on the right side of the vehicle away from the cars.

F   13-29. Intensive, representative, and minimum showings are used when buying exterior displays.

T   13-30. The uses of transit advertising vary with the importance of the transit system in the market area.

Multiple Choice

B   13-31. The following are classified as standardized outdoor advertising except:
  A. Bulletins
  B. Roadside signs
  C. Posters
  D. Two of the above
  E. All or none of the above

A   13-32. Which of the following is not classified as outdoor advertising?
  A. Exterior displays
  B. Posters
  C. Advertising spectaculars
  D. On-premise signs
  E. None of the above

C   13-33. Which statement concerning advertising spectaculars is false?
  A. It is considered "permanent" as it will not be moved on a rotation basis.
  B. It is a nonstandardized form of outdoor mobile media.
  C. It is inexpensive when compared with other types of outdoor advertising.
  D. It is placed at a high traffic location in a major city.
  E. It has an expected life span of 3-5 years.

C 13-34. The standard billboard, which involves a proportion of 2¼ to 1, has a frame size of:
A. 19'6" x 8'8"
B. 21'7" x 9'7"
C. 22'8" x 10'5"
D. 30'9" x 15'3"
E. 48' x 14'

B 13-35. The 24-sheet and 30-sheet advertising poster is now typically printed on:
A. 8 and 10 sheets respectively
B. 10 and 14 sheets respectively
C. 12 and 15 sheets respectively
D. 16 and 20 sheets respectively
E. 10 and 10 sheets respectively

D 13-36. A bleed poster:
A. Uses all of the blanking area as part of the poster
B. Uses a copy area of 21'7" x 9'7".
C. Uses 40% more copy area than a 24 sheet poster
D. Two of the above are used
E. All of the above are used

B 13-37. Which of the following is a disadvantage of using outdoor mobile media?
A. Market selectivity
B. Image
C. Cost
D. Reach/frequency
E. Size

A 13-38. As a general rule, outdoor advertising should not be used, unless the advertising message consists of:
A. Six words or less
B. Nine words or less
C. Twelve words or less
D. Eighteen words or less
E. Twenty words or less

D 13-39. When choosing a preferred position for his/her outdoor advertisement, an advertiser would consider all the following except:
A. Traffic speed
B. Board angle
C. Circulation
D. Copy length
E. Length of approach

D 13-40. A billboard that is parallel to the road is best for:
A. Traffic on a curve
B. Vehicle traffic from both directions
C. Pedestrian traffic
D. Two of the above
E. All of the above

C   13-41.   An outdoor advertiser who wishes to obtain daily exposures equal to the population, would buy enough posters to obtain:
   A.   50 gross rating points
   B.   A 50 showing
   C.   100 gross rating points
   D.   A 100 showing
   E.   None of the above

B   13-42.   The outdoor industry changed its unit of measure in 1973 from a showing to:
   A.   An exposure
   B.   A gross rating point
   C.   A reach
   D.   A frequency
   E.   None of the above

E   13-43.   An audience measurement study for outdoor media conducted by W. R. Simmons revealed that:
   A.   Outdoor advertising reaches almost all adults in professional or managerial occupations
   B.   89.2% of all adults were reached in 30 days
   C.   96% of adults who attended college were reached
   D.   The frequency rate was 31 times
   E.   All of the above

D   13-44.   The audience study measurement for outdoor media undertaken by Target Group Index in 1975, revealed that:
   A.   92% of adults 18-34 years old are reached
   B.   A high income person ($25,000 or more) is more likely to "see" outdoor ads then T.V., radio, newspapers, or magazines
   C.   Outdoor advertising has the least potential reach for the low income consumer
   D.   Two of the above
   E.   All of the above

D   13-45.   All of the following are uses of outdoor advertising except:
   A.   Outdoor can be supportive, that is, a reinforcement vehicle
   B.   Outdoor can be a way to reach the masses
   C.   Outdoor can be an impulse generator
   D.   All of the above are uses
   E.   None of the above are uses

B   13-46.   The Transit Advertising Association has standardized the size of car cards so that most cards are:
   A.   8 inches high
   B.   11 inches high
   C.   22 inches high
   D.   28 inches high
   E.   42 inches high

E 13-47. Advertising impact can be achieved in transit advertising by all the
following methods except:
A. Buying a total-total bus
B. Purchasing a large-sized ad
C. Painting the vehicle to resemble a product
D. Buying all the ads inside or outside of the bus
E. All of the above promote advertising impact

A 13-48. Transit advertising in smaller metropolitan areas should not be aimed at:
A. Businessmen
B. The elderly
C. Domestic help
D. Children
E. All of the above

C 13-49. Preferred positions for an ad inside a bus include all the following except:
A. Facing the seats over the wheels
B. By the doors
C. Above the back seat
D. Near the front
E. None of the above

B 13-50. Station displays are purchased in units which are called:
A. Service values
B. Showings
C. Gross rating points
D. CUMEs
E. None of the above

Completion

13-51. (*Mobile*) media is often referred to as "out-of-home" media because it is
used to drive a message home to a customer who is not at home.

13-52. Mobile media consists of (*transit*) media and (*outdoor*) media.

13-53. The term "billboard," which dates back to the 19th century when companies
began leasing space on wooden boards for advertising messages called "bills,"
is a common term for a (*poster*).

13-54. The two major types of bulletins that are available to an advertiser are
the (*embellished*) bulletin and the (*trivision*) bulletin.

13-55. The (*Traffic Audit Bureau*) is an organization that provides audience
measurement data for posters and bulletins.

13-56. (*Transit advertising*) delivers an advertising message to people who are
traveling by means other than their own vehicle and/or uses public vehicles
or structures as places to affix ads to reach the general public.

13-57. Transit advertisements which are 11 inches high and either 21, 28, 42, or
56 inches long are known as (*car cards*).

13-58. An advertiser who purchases the entire interior of a bus for display
purposes is buying a (*basic bus*) or a Moods in Motion.

13-59. A (_total-total bus_) refers to an advertiser's purchase of all the ad space outside and inside the bus.

13-60. The purchase unit for exterior display is a (_showing_), while car cards are purchased in units called (_service values_).

CHAPTER 14 - POINT-OF-PURCHASE
AND OTHER MEDIA

True or False

F   14-1. In a "closed-back" window display, the interior of the building becomes, to a certain degree, a part of the display.

F   14-2. A window display should be changed at least every five days in order to keep the window distinctive and attention-getting.

T   14-3. A wall display may be a clock featuring a product manufacturer's logo, a menu sign, or any sign that aids in identifying the manufacturer or retailer.

T   14-4. The "cut-out" display, unlike the merchandise rack, is not normally of a permanent design.

T   14-5. A talking or audio-visual display can be used to explain a product's benefits, but it loses effectiveness when too many are in use in a given location.

F   14-6. The success of a vending machine display is dependent upon its contents, as is true with most point-of-purchase displays.

T   14-7. The package as well as the product itself serve as forms of point-of-purchase display.

T   14-8. A point-of-purchase display, acting as a nonperson salesperson, should attempt to sell a product.

F   14-9. According to the Robinson-Patman Act, an advertiser who offers to buy display space in one store is not legally bound to offer to buy space in other stores on a proportional basis.

T   14-10. Studies show that point-of-purchase advertising does attract customers to the product which results in increased sales, especially for items marketed in a self-service environment.

F   14-11. Local and national advertisers together spend approximately $2.5 billion annually on point-of-purchase displays.

T   14-12. As the greatest user of point-of-purchase displays on the local level, the retail store uses both ready-made and in-house created displays.

T   14-13. An advertising specialty item must be both useful and unique in the eyes of the recipient in order to promote ad impressions.

T   14-14. Personalized business gifts are very popular in the business market, though they are limited as to the amount of advertising on the item.

F 14-15. Regardless of the specialty item used, the life span of the ad message does not exceed the life expectancy of any other media.

F 14-16. Specialty advertising is limited by size and time allowed to get the message across, thus making it a medium with little flexibility.

T 14-17. The limited space for advertising copy that is available on pens, pencils, etc. can be overcome somewhat by making creative use of the available space.

T 14-18. Specialty advertising can be distributed to a select group or to the masses depending on the advertiser's needs.

T 14-19. Studies show that specialty advertising is viewed favorably by both the consumer audience and the business audience.

F 14-20. Firms are not allowed to list their business name under more than three headings in the Yellow Pages consumer directory, but they can choose the type of listing they want.

T 14-21. The permanence aspect of the Yellow Pages directory advertisement is a disadvantage to the firm that moves or changes its phone number.

F 14-22. Businesses that deal in urgency or have a high level of brand loyalty may not benefit from advertising in the Yellow Pages directory.

T 14-23. The National Yellow Pages Service permits an advertiser to buy all the directories that are needed without dealing with the individual phone companies.

T 14-24. The target market and type of business along with cost should determine if the advertiser should place an ad in the Yellow Pages.

F 14-26. Theatrical advertising is not advertising in the traditional sense, since it does not look like advertising to the viewer.

F 14-27. The advertiser can expect nontheatrical advertising to serve some long-term corporate goals while also providing short-term sales impact.

F 14-28. Donation advertising, like all advertising, should be expected to generate sales.

T 14-29. The purpose of donation advertising is goodwill and public relations, and as such should not be treated as part of the advertising budget.

F 14-30. The terms "specialty advertising" and "advertising specialties" are synonymous and can, therefore, be used interchangeably.

Multiple Choice

D 14-31. Point-of-purchase advertising is sometimes referred to as:
A. Point-of-sale display
B. Dealer aid
C. Dealer display
D. All of the above
E. None of the above

134

D   14-32.   Which of the following is not classified as a form of point-of-purchase advertising?
A. Display cards
B. Vending machines
C. Cut-outs
D. Impulse displays
E. Merchandise racks

A   14-33.   For purposes of classification, window displays may be classified in several ways. Which one is not a widely used window classification?
A. A full-dressed window
B. A public service window
C. A promotional window
D. An institutional window
E. All or none of the above

B   14-34.   Which of the following is not an advantage of point-of-purchase advertising?
A. It reinforces other promotional efforts
B. It promotes repeat buying
C. It encourages the unplanned purchase
D. It works in a self-service environment
E. None of the above

E   14-35.   The impact of a point-of-purchase display can be improved upon in all of the following ways except by using:
A. Motion
B. Lights
C. Bright colors
D. Exciting artwork
E. None of the above

A   14-36.   The buying-habits study cited in the text revealed that the following number of supermarket purchases were unplanned or impulse purchases:
A. Almost one out of two
B. Almost one out of three
C. Almost one out of four
D. Almost one out of five
E. Almost one out of ten

C   14-37.   All of the following statements concerning the design of a point-of-purchase display are true except:
A. Since a good display is difficult to develop, design is viewed as a disadvantage.
B. The design should integrate the product into the display.
C. The display should be attractive enough to draw the customer to the display, even make the customer want the display.
D. The display should be creative.
E. The display should be a selling tool.

C 14-38. The average supermarket in the Point-of-Purchase/DuPont Survey was found to have _____ end-aisle or special-unit displays as well as _____ display items featured elsewhere in the store.
A. 45.9, 60.7
B. 72.1, 105.3
C. 63.5, 159.9
D. 86.8, 174.2
E. 101.4, 212.6

B 14-39. According to the Point-of-Purchase Advertising Institute, the four I's of point-of-purchase advertising are:
A. Impact, Interest, Information, Identification
B. Impact, Information, Imagery, Identification
C. Impact, Interest, Inducement, Identification
D. Interest, Inducement, Inspect, Impact
E. None of the above

E 14-40. A definition of specialty advertising would not include the following element:
A. Advertiser's imprint or logo
B. No-obligation distribution
C. Useful article of merchandise
D. Two of the above
E. All of the above are included in the definition

A 14-41. Which of the following is not a part of specialty advertising according to the text:
A. Novelty items
B. Advertising calendars
C. Advertising specialties
D. Business gifts
E. None of the above

E 14-42. Which of the following is not a characteristic of an advertising specialty?
A. The items are nominal in dollar value
B. The items bear the advertiser's identity
C. The items are well suited for general distribution
D. The items are useful
E. None of the above

D 14-43. The advertising calendar is not classified as an advertising specialty because:
A. They may be expensive (not nominal in value)
B. They may be limited as to the amount of advertising on them
C. They are often given as gifts
D. Two of the above
E. All of the above

D 14-44. The disadvantage(s) of using specialty advertising is/are:
A. Longevity
B. Advertising cost
C. Limited copy space
D. Two of the above
E. All of the above

136

B   14-45. A disadvantage of Yellow Page advertising is:
             A. Availability
             B. Customer usage
             C. Directionality
             D. Permanence
             E. None of the above

E   14-46. The following businesses benefit from Yellow Page advertising:
             A. Businesses dealing in urgency
             B. Restaurants
             C. Businesses having a high level of brand loyalty
             D. Firms that have business generated by phone
             E. All of the above

A   14-47. A disadvantage of theatrical advertising is:
             A. Reach
             B. Demographic selectivity
             C. Impact
             D. Geographic selectivity
             E. All of the above

B   14-48. Which of the following is not a primary application for specialty advertising
             as cited by the Specialty Advertising Association's list of uses?
             A. Building an image
             B. Encouraging impulse buying
             C. Promoting a grand opening
             D. Introducing new salesmen
             E. Balancing an improper product mix

E   14-49. The use of a Yellow Page directory by an advertiser should not be determined
             by:
             A. The potential benefit
             B. Type of business
             C. Cost
             D. Target market
             E. All of the above should help determine usage

E   14-50. Which of the following is not an advertising medium?
             A. Business cards
             B. A banner pulled by a plane
             C. Clothing worn by personnel featuring the company logo
             D. Product image projected on a building
             E. All are advertising media

Completion

14-51. The three forms of specialty advertising are (*advertising specialties*),
        (*advertising calendars*), and (*business gifts*).

14-52. Known as remembrance advertising, (*point-of-purchase*) ads are located at
        or near the point of sale.

14-53. The primary function of the sign in front of a place of business, called an
        (*on-premise*) sign, is identification.

14-54. The function of an (*institutional*) window display is to sell the firm; while the (*promotional*) window display sells the merchandise. On the other hand, a (*public service*) window display is a goodwill venture that should not be charged to the advertising budget.

14-55. A point-of-purchase advertiser must minimize the problems related to (*clutter*), (*placement*), and (*design*), if the firm's displays are to be effective.

14-56. There are two types of screen advertising: (*theatrical*) and (*nontheatrical*).

14-57. The four I's of point-of-purchase advertising are: (*identification*), (*imagery*), (*impact*), and (*information*).

14-58. The Revenue Act of 1962 limits tax-deductable business gifts to (*$25*) per year per person but excludes imprinted advertising specialties costing (*$4*) or less.

14-59. The advantages of specialty advertising are (*flexibility*), (*longevity*), and (*selectivity*).

14-60. The disadvantages of Yellow Page directory advertising are (*market coverage*), or limited access, and (*customer usage*).

CHAPTER 15 - ADVERTISING BUDGET

True or False

F   15-1. The advertising appropriation shows how much will be spent in the various media that are used by a firm.

T   15-2. A firm's failure to budget its advertising can lead to problems since it may use up its advertising appropriation too soon or spend too much on advertising.

T   15-3. Budgeting tends to reduce mistakes while increasing the value of the advertising program as a result of planning.

T   15-4. A budget may include projected results of the ads to be run for which the advertising personnel are held accountable.

F   15-5. The popular methods that are used to determine the advertising appropriation for a company yield a figure that is both useful and reliable.

F   15-6. The unit-of-sale method of determining the advertising budget is the most popular as well as simple appropriation method in use.

F   15-7. An advertiser who imitates his competition's advertising - that is, uses the competitive-parity appropriation method - is following a safe path for determining the advertising appropriation.

T   15-8. The all-you-can-afford appropriation method deals with what a firm can afford to spend on advertising.

T   15-9.   To maintain or increase market share, the advertising share should exceed the market share under the market-share method of advertising appropriation.

T   15-10. Many of the advertising appropriation methods ignore the quality of the advertising, the other parts of the marketing mix, and the role that advertising plays in relation to personal selling.

F   15-11. The market-share appropriation method builds an advertising budget based on a foundation of objectives.

T   15-12. The task method forces the advertiser to think through his/her advertising needs in greater depth than any of the other appropriation methods.

F   15-13. According to the San Augustine-Foley study of appropriation methods, 20 percent of the consumer firms in the sample used quantitative models in their appropriation decision.

T   15-14. The communication-stage model for determining the advertising appropriation is a complex procedure that requires the use of least-squares regression techniques.

F   15-15. The competitive-share model for determining the advertising allocation applies continuing test-market procedures to keep the sales-response function up-to-date.

T   15-16. The best approach for appropriating advertising funds is to use a combination of qualitative and quantitative methods.

T   15-17. Budget attrition, the tendency to cover expenses that are not advertising with the advertising allocation, dilutes the funds available for advertising.

T   15-18. An understanding of the stages of the product life cycle will influence how a firm budgets its advertising.

F   15-19. Competition should be ignored as an influence in determining the advertising budget.

F   15-20. The smaller store in a mall location generally spends more on advertising rather than paying for it indirectly with its rent payment.

F   15-21. One of the more difficult budget allocation procedures involves the geographic allocation of funds.

T   15-22. The advertising budget should provide funds for the duration of the fiscal period.

T   15-23. To assure the proper allocation of the advertising budget, the fiscal period should be divided into budgeting units which consider special promotions as well as the normal passage of time.

T   15-24. For budgeting purposes, the advertising effort should be divided up into regions just as a major firm is divided up in terms of organization.

F   15-25. The advertising budget allocation should be determined by the product life cycle and competition.

F   15-26. A good budget is a plan of action that should be followed as planned with no deviations permitted because none will be required.

T   15-27. Due to changes in the factors that influence the advertising budget, procedures should be set up that permit deviations from the budgeted plan of action.

F   15-28. According to the Internal Revenue Service (IRS), advertising is a capital investment.

F   15-29. A firm that is using a sales-response and decay model assumes that the curve is convex from the beginning which means that additional advertising will always yield diminishing returns.

T   15-30. Due to changing market conditions, adaptive-control models apply test-market procedures on a continuing basis with different levels of advertising effort in each test market area.

Multiple Choice

B   15-31. Which of the following statements concerning a firm's advertising budget is false?
A. The budget tells how much the firm will spend on advertising in July.
B. The budget is easier to develop than the appropriation.
C. The budget is a detailed plan about how to spend the advertising money.
D. The budget determines how much to spend on advertising.
E. None of the above

C   15-32. Which of the following methods of determining the advertising appropriation is not a common method?
A. Competitive-parity method
B. Unit-of-sale method
C. Zero-base method
D. Market-share method
E. Arbitrary method

E   15-33. Which statement concerning the percentage-of-sales advertising appropriation method is false?
A. The method may use forecasted sales or historical data.
B. A study of major consumer advertisers showed 50% used a percentage of anticipated sales procedure for determining their appropriation.
C. The method may be a cop-out for the advertiser.
D. The amount of advertising depends on the level of sales.
E. None of the above.

E   15-34. According to the observations of J. O. Peckham of the A. C. Nielsen Co., which statement is false?
A. For new products, the advertising share should double expected market share.
B. The advertising share should be greater than expected market share to increase market share.
C. The advertising share should be greater than expected market share to maintain market share.
D. There is a relationship between market share and advertising share.
E. None of the above are false.

140

B   15-35.   All but one of the following methods of determining the advertising
               appropriation set an amount to spend on advertising without first determining
               how much advertising is actually needed. That one method is the:
               A.   All-you-can-afford method
               B.   Task method
               C.   Percentage-of-sales method
               D.   Market-share method
               E.   Competitive-parity method

D   15-36.   Of the following, which is a quantitative method of setting the advertising
               appropriation?
               A.   Competitive-parity model
               B.   Competitive-share model
               C.   Sales-response and decay model
               D.   Two of the above
               E.   All of the above

E   15-37.   The sales-response and decay model may assume that:
               A.   The advertising sales response function is concave from the beginning
               B.   The shape of the sales-response-to-advertising curve is known
               C.   Additional advertising will always yield diminishing returns
               D.   Two of the above
               E.   All of the above

C   15-38.   Which of the following statements is true about the percentage-of-sales
               method for determining the advertising appropriation:
               A.   The method is not widely used.
               B.   The method usually results in an appropriation that is not obtainable
                    unless adjustments are made.
               C.   The method can use either past sales or future sales or a composite
                    of the two as the figure upon which to determine the appropriation.
               D.   The method is very popular since it allows the advertiser to make
                    automatic adjustments for budget attrition.
               E.   None of the above

C   15-39.   An advertising budget model is a:
               A.   Decision maker
               B.   "Cop-out" device
               C.   Decision tool
               D.   All of the above
               E.   None of the above

A   15-40.   According to Printers' Ink, all of the following charges should be included
               in the advertising budget except:
               A.   Market research
               B.   Ad pretesting
               C.   Direct mail
               D.   Space and time costs in regular media
               E.   All of the above

B 15-41. The following factor(s) would not be considered in determining the amount that should be placed in a certain account within the advertising budget:
A. Competition
B. Controllable internal factors
C. Promotional strategy
D. Product life cycle
E. Uncontrollable external restraints

E 15-42. The product life cycle (PLC) affects the advertising budget because:
A. An established product requires less advertising to maintain market share
B. Taking an existing product for granted may move it into a premature sales decline
C. In the PLC introduction stage, you need high promotional expenditures
D. It costs money to establish a new product
E. All of the above

B 15-43. Competition should:
A. Determine the size of the advertising budget
B. Influence the advertising budget
C. Be matched dollar for dollar in the advertising budget
D. Two of the above
E. All of the above

E 15-44. Which factor is not considered when allocating the advertising budget?
A. Media
B. Geography
C. Product/service
D. Time
E. All or none of the above

D 15-45. Which of the following statement(s) concerning the product/service budget allocation is/are false?
A. The needs of the total organization must be considered.
B. Care should be taken to insure that all budgets are coordinated for the total good of the company.
C. Care should be taken to avoid duplication of effort and expense.
D. All statements are true.
E. All statements are false.

C 15-46. The rule of thumb for how much variance is permissable in the advertising budget without managerial action is:
A. 1%
B. 3%
C. 5%
D. 10%
E. None of the above

A 15-47. The cumulative effect of advertising does not:
A. Promote the idea of advertising as a short term expense
B. Allow each ad to build on the last ad as well as all past ads
C. Give a current ad more clout
D. Promote the idea of advertising as an investment
E. None of the above

142

A   15-48. According to Printers' Ink, the group of charges that may or may not be
            included in the advertising budget depending on the situation would include
            all of the following except:
            A. Customer entertainment
            B. Exhibit costs
            C. Contest awards
            D. Dealer literature
            E. All or none of the above

E   15-49. A benefit of budgeting your advertising is that:
            A. It makes the person in charge of advertising accountable for the results
            B. It promotes efficiency
            C. It forces planning
            D. It makes the person in charge of advertising accountable for ad placement
            E. All of the above

C   15-50. The advertising budget should be viewed as a:
            A. Planning device
            B. Control device
            C. Planning and control device
            D. Academic exercise that is not necessary in the real world
            E. Attrition device

                                    Completion

15-51. The advertising (*appropriation*) for a firm is the lump sum amount to be
        spent on advertising.

15-52. A firm's detailed plan on how its advertising appropriation will be spent is
        called its advertising (*budget*).

15-53. The benefits to the advertiser of setting up a budget include (*planning*),
        (*accountability*), and (*efficiency*).

15-54. The most popular method of determining the advertising appropriation is the
        (*percentage-of-sales*) method which has simplicity as its greatest benefit.

15-55. The advertising appropriation method that determines the budget in relation
        to the units sold or to be sold is called the (*unit-of-sale*) method. This
        method has received wide use with farm products.

15-56. The goal of (*sales-response and decay*) models is the determination of the
        optimum point of advertising outlay on the sales-response curve.

15-57. A/an (*communication-stage*) model derives the budget size by noting its
        effects on several intermediate variables that link sales and advertising
        expenditures while assuming a multi-level ad effort.

15-58. The (*competitive-parity*) appropriation method, or followship, assumes that
        the competitor is making the right decisions and that the competitor's
        operation is similar to the advertiser's.

15-59. Under the market-share method of advertising appropriation, if a firm projects
        the sales for its new product to be 30 percent of the total market, then its
        share of total industry advertising effort should be (*60*) percent.

15-60. Factors that influence the size of the advertising budget are: (*product life cycle*), (*competition*), (*promotional strategy*), and (*uncontrollable external restraints*).

CHAPTER 16 - MEDIA PLAN

True or False

T 16-1. A media plan is a blue print of a firm's forthcoming advertising program; that is, it is a detailed plan of action dealing with how to reach the target market through advertising.

F 16-2. The less precise or quantified the media objectives of a firm, the better the objectives.

T 16-3. To develop the media plan, the media objectives must be translated into workable guidelines that help in the selection of media.

F 16-4. Media strategies provide the information that fills in the details of the media plan.

F 16-5. The advertising budget provides the upper and lower dollar limits on the media plan.

T 16-6. Media discounts, if considered carefully, can be a positive influence on the media plan.

F 16-7. Due to the new media buying models, media efficiency no longer influences the media plan.

T 16-8. A firm's policy of always taking action in response to a competitor's advertising requires a high level of flexibility in the media plan.

T 16-9. A major change in the promotion mix (advertising, sales promotion, personal selling, and publicity) may require a complete rethinking of the media plan.

T 16-10. A national coverage media plan strives to reach as much of the population as possible at the lowest possible CPM.

F 16-11. TV Guide magazine is a logical media choice for a skim coverage media plan.

T 16-12. Key-market media plans allow for media flexibility so that local testimonials or local features may be added.

F 16-13. Key-market coverage campaigns can be different from area to area since coordination of the different advertising programs is not important.

T 16-14. A skim media strategy often starts with a prestige market, and then moves down the economic/social ladder.

F 16-15. A skim media strategy is the most popular coverage plan since competitors can be easily handled.

144

F   16-16.   The goal of a reach media strategy is to promote awareness, interest, and desire for the product.

T   16-17.   A continuity media strategy is being followed when slogans, trade characters, logos, or jingles are carried forward to the new ad campaign from the old one.

T   16-18.   Once the advertiser determines which media would be the best to use to fit the firm's needs, the next task is to select the best scheduling or media-placement tactic.

T   16-19.   Due to limited funds, a dominance media strategy is hard to maintain when the steady schedule media tactic is adopted.

F   16-20.   The seasonal schedule media tactic borrows from the steady and the alternating tactics by providing a steady stream of ads for a few weeks, then stops for a few weeks, before the cycle begins again.

T   16-21.   The seasonal media schedule is similar to pulsing except that each flight of ads is tied to the seasonal selling cycle of the product.

T   16-22.   When determining the media schedule for a firm, the advertiser should realize that not all media permit certain types of scheduling and that media discount schedules may not match the proposed scheduling plans.

T   16-23.   The iteration model for media planning involves repetition of instructions and a set of rules to identify the best solution. It is attractive to advertisers since the thought process is automated once the model is set up.

F   16-24.   The most beneficial aspect of iteration is that it yields an optimum solution while considering the effect of past advertising.

F   16-25.   A heuristic rule that is used by an advertiser is assumed to be true in all cases.

F   16-26.   The assumptions used in a simulation model do not need to match the advertiser's target market in order to be effective in selecting media.

T   16-27.   Computer models can play an important role in media plan development so long as they don't replace the advertiser's judgement.

F   16-28.   The rate of advertising carryover decay does not vary between sales-price advertising and institutional advertising.

F   16-29.   The advertising impact for institutional advertising is minimal after one month from the date of ad placement.

T   16-30.   Though media buying is a major task, the smart advertiser takes the time to learn from other advertisers what they pay for similar buys before confronting the media.

145

Multiple Choice

C   16-31. An advertiser who is developing a media plan should consider all the
             following except:
             A. The cumulative effect of advertising
             B. Media strategy
             C. The budget attrition appropriation
             D. The plan components
             E. None of the above

A   16-32. The greatest benefit or asset to the firm of media planning is:
             A. A well-planned coordinated system of media utilization designed
                 to give the best results for the given budget
             B. That no further work is needed for a year
             C. That you can ignore sales calls from media representatives
             D. The detailed media schedule
             E. All or none of the above

B   16-33. The foundation of a media plan consists of knowledge concerning which
             of the following areas?
                 I.   Reach or frequency levels   IV. Competition
                 II. Ad placement   V.   Media characteristics
                 III. Copy and layout   VI. Target market

             A. I, III, V, VI
             B. III, IV, V, VI
             C. II, IV, V, VI
             D. I, II, III, V
             E. II, III, IV, V

E   16-34. Which of the following statements concerning the media buying component of
             the media plan is false?
             A. The advertiser wants to be sure money was not spent on ads that were not
                 run or were run incorrectly.
             B. The advertising purchases of an advertiser are important to the firm.
             C. Follow-up is needed to evaluate the ads for their effect on sales and
                 traffic.
             D. A media plan without follow-up may be ineffective.
             E. None of the above are false.

C   16-35. Which of the following is the correct chain of events in a media plan?
             A. Media objectives - Media strategy - Marketing objectives -
                 Marketing strategy - Media tactics - Media buying
             B. Marketing strategy - Marketing objectives - Media strategy -
                 Media objectives - Media buying - Media tactics
             C. Marketing objectives - Marketing strategy - Media objectives -
                 Media strategy - Media tactics - Media buying
             D. Media tactics - Media strategies - Media objectives -
                 Marketing strategies - Marketing objectives - Media buying
             E. None of the above

E   16-36. Each individual situation will determine how the media plan will be altered by such factors as:
A. The promotion mix
B. The budget size
C. The media discount structures
D. The nature of the product
E. All or none of the above

B   16-37. Which of the following is not a media allocation plan that would result from a coverage strategy decision by the media planner?
A. Key-market plan
B. Regional plan
C. Skim plan
D. National plan
E. All or none of the above

D   16-38. The logical media choice(s) for a national coverage plan are:
A. Mass-oriented magazines
B. Direct mail
C. Network television and radio
D. Two of the above
E. All of the above

E   16-39. The area covered by a key-market coverage strategy is a:
A. Region
B. ADI
C. Geographic area
D. State
E. May be any of the above

A   16-40. The media choices for a key-market coverage strategy include all of the following except:
A. National network radio
B. Spot radio
C. Regional or special edition magazines
D. Spot television
E. All or none of the above

B   16-41. The "trickle down" media strategy is another name for the:
A. Key-market media plan
B. Skim media plan
C. Coverage media plan
D. National media plan
E. None of the above

E   16-42. The skim media strategy attempts to market to:
A. A special group of customers with a particular interest
B. One particular market
C. A prestige market first, then sells to markets lower down on the social/economic ladder until each market is sold
D. Two of the above
E. All of the above

D   16-43.   In terms of media strategy, continuity means that:
                 A.   The ads for one firm are run throughout a program
                 B.   Successful campaigns should be continued with each new campaign building on the last one's successful components
                 C.   When customers continue hearing about a firm, they begin to remember the advertiser
                 D.   Two of the above
                 E.   All of the above

A   16-44.   The <u>Timex</u> commercial that uses a torture test on the watch is using the media strategy known as:
                 A.   Continuity
                 B.   Skimming
                 C.   Frequency
                 D.   Dominance
                 E.   Coverage

E   16-45.   An advertiser can dominate the advertising environment by using:
                 A.   Bigger ads
                 B.   Preferred positions
                 C.   Longer commercials
                 D.   Color and bleed ads
                 E.   All or none of the above

C   16-46.   An advertiser can promote dominance on a limited budget by using the _____ schedule media tactic.
                 A.   Alternating-even
                 B.   Steady
                 C.   Alternating-staggered
                 D.   Only A and C
                 E.   All of the above

B   16-47.   An advertiser can use any of the following models to aid him/her in selecting and scheduling media except:
                 A.   Heuristic programming
                 B.   Pulsing
                 C.   Iteration
                 D.   Simulation
                 E.   Linear programming

E   16-48.   Linear programming procedures attempt to allocate a scarce resource among different uses to obtain optimum usage. Along with its strong points, problems are inherent in its methodology. One of these problems is that it:
                 A.   Does not state when the ads should be scheduled
                 B.   Assumes that repeat exposures have a constant marginal effect
                 C.   Cannot handle the problem of audience duplication
                 D.   Assumes constant media costs and no media discounts
                 E.   All or none of the above

B   16-49.   As a media-planning model, MEDIAC is an example of:
                 A.   Simulation
                 B.   Heuristic programming
                 C.   Linear programming
                 D.   Iteration
                 E.   None of the above

C   16-50.   Pulsing, or grouping ads in flights, calls for an advertiser to provide a steady stream of ads for _____ weeks followed by no ads for _____ weeks.
              A. Four, two
              B. Six, two
              C. Four, four
              D. Six, four
              E. Six, six

Completion

16-51.   The process of designing a course of action that shows how advertising time and space will be used to contribute to the achievement of marketing objectives is called (*media planning*).

16-52.   The heart of the media plan is the (*media objectives*) or goals which are dependent on the marketing objectives and marketing strategies of the firm.

16-53.   (*Media tactics*) are the ways that the media strategies are implemented.

16-54.   A firm's (*media strategy*) should consist of guidelines that will be followed to implement the media objectives or goals.

16-55.   The media strategy for a (*national*) plan strives for complete coverage -- reaching the masses.

16-56.   The (*skim*) coverage media plan, like the (*key-market*) media plan does not strive for complete coverage, but it does aim at a demographic or psychographic perspective rather than a geographic one.

16-57.   If mass exposure, or a/an (*reach*) strategy is desired, a multi-media mix will most likely be pursued. On the other hand, repetition will be most important if a/an (*frequency*) strategy is desired, and the choice of media will not be as great.

16-58.   (*Continuity*) of advertising provides the same benefit as repetition; and if done well, it will allow the ads of the firm to reenforce themselves over time for the benefit of the advertiser.

16-59.   An (*alternating-even*) media tactic places ads of the same length or size at regular intervals (every two days, every week, etc.). The (*alternating-staggered*) schedule, on the other hand, varies the size or length of the ads that are run at the regular interval.

16-60.   A (*heuristic*) rule is a decision rule of thumb that can be programmed into a computer by an advertiser as an aid in media selection and scheduling.

CHAPTER 17 - ADVERTISING RESEARCH AND EVALUATION

True or False

F   17-1.   Advertising research, as a part of marketing research, is defined as the gathering, recording, and analyzing of data about problems relating to the marketing of goods and services.

T   17-2.   Advertising research is sometimes referred to as copy testing.

T   17-3.   Advertising research can prevent the advertiser from making costly mistakes.

T   17-4.   Although it is difficult to measure the effect of advertising, many firms use advertising research on a routine, on-going basis.

F   17-5.   In terms of research, a firm's declining sales would normally be defined as the problem rather than as a symptom of the problem.

F   17-6.   Primary data is information that has been collected by another source that is used to solve an advertiser's problem.

F   17-7.   In most cases, an advertiser needing current data can rely on secondary data sources for the information.

T   17-8.   Nonprobability samples are easy to obtain, inexpensive, and subject to error.

F   17-9.   When a nonprobability sample is taken, the advertiser can statistically project the findings of the study to the population.

T   17-10. The sample is as important in research as the method that is used.

T   17-11. One major weakness of the observation method of data collection is that it waits for something to happen, but this is also its major advantage in that no artificial stimulus is used to force a person to act.

F   17-12. The most popular form of primary data collection is the observation technique.

T   17-13. An advertiser who is using a mail survey should be aware of the silent majority who simply will not respond.

F   17-14. As a means of data collection, the telephone is the most popular form of survey technique since it is a low-cost means of reaching many people in a short time period.

T   17-15. People are often suspicious of telephone surveys because so many sales people have used a "survey" to get the customer's attention on the phone.

F   17-16. In advertising research, statistical analysis is always necessary in data analysis.

T   17-17. Firms that spend their time and money on advertising research should act promptly on the findings in order to avoid making decisions that are based on dated information.

T   17-18. In a projective pretest, the respondent is asked to assume another person's identity because it is felt that more truthful answers will be given than if the person is asked a question outright.

T   17-19. Depending on the purpose of a ranking pretest, the ads shown to a respondent may be very similar or quite different.

150

F   17-20.   The semantic differential technique and the Likert scale are commonly used by advertising researchers for pretest-projective studies.

T   17-21.   Attitudes are difficult to measure because they are intangible and can change very rapidly.

T   17-22.   Proponents of brain pattern analysis feel that this is an effective technique for pretesting ads because brain waves indicate how people really respond to commercials.

F   17-23.   The eye tracking pretest technique measures the change in the diameter of the pupil of the eye as a respondent receives a visual stimulus.

T   17-24.   The recognition posttest technique becomes more valid for an advertiser's use when the study is expanded by time and number of ads.

F   17-25.   The recall posttest technique is effective in measuring the impact of an ad but it cannot be used to measure a campaign's effectiveness.

F   17-26.   In both the recognition technique and the recall technique of posttest ad evaluation, the known reader of a magazine is shown an advertisement before being asked to talk about it.

F   17-27.   The ad generating the most inquiries in a posttest ad evaluation should be chosen by the advertiser as the best ad.

T   17-28.   The direct media can be used effectively to measure the drawing power of an ad under either the sales technique or inquiry technique of posttest advertising evaluation.

F   17-29.   When using a test vs. control posttest technique, an advertiser can study the effect of several variables on the market at one time.

F   17-30.   Customer diaries are costly to use but this posttest technique provides the advertiser with very accurate data.

Multiple Choice

D   17-31.   Advertising research deals with:
          A.   Message analysis
          B.   Target Market analysis
          C.   Media analysis
          D.   Two of the above
          E.   All of the above

E   17-32.   Of the following, which is not a disadvantage of advertising research?
          A.   Research can cause a delay which could prevent a product/service/idea from being marketed on time
          B.   The advertiser has no true measure of advertising effectiveness
          C.   Research costs time and money
          D.   Two of the above are disadvantages
          E.   All of the above are disadvantages

E 17-33. James Wallace's five-step approach for measuring advertising's contribution to marketing illustrates:
A. A major disadvantage of advertising research
B. The frustrations felt by those working in advertising research
C. The difficulty of separating a firm's advertising from the other marketing elements
D. Two of the above
E. All of the above

B 17-34. In order to improve on the advantages of advertising research, the researcher should employ all the following steps of the research process except:
A. Data analysis
B. Budget allocation
C. Primary and secondary data collection
D. Problem definition
E. Data presentation and follow-up

A 17-35. Secondary data is least likely to come from which source?
A. Experimentation
B. A. C. Nielsen
C. Internal sources
D. The government
E. None of the above

D 17-36. Primary data may be collected by means of:
A. Experimentation
B. Survey
C. Sampling
D. Two of the above
E. All of the above

E 17-37. Another name for the nonprobability sampling approach is:
A. Quota sample
B. Judgement sample
C. Convenience sample
D. Both A and C
E. All of the above

D 17-38. Which of the following statements concerning a mail survey is false?
A. It may lead to highly biased responses.
B. The use of a postage-free return envelope makes it a quick way to gather data.
C. It is a convenient and economical way to obtain information.
D. Both B and C
E. Both A and B

E 17-39. As a means of data collection, a personal interview is not popular due to:
A. Potential interviewer bias
B. Cost
C. Physical danger to the interviewer in many locations
D. Two of the above
E. All of the above

E   17-40. The experimentation data collection technique would least likely be used to
             test:
             A. Different package designs
             B. Different point-of-purchase displays
             C. Various advertising campaigns
             D. Different media mixes
             E. All or none of the above

B   17-41. The DAGMAR evaluation method for advertising does not provide the user with:
             A. Guidance for ad creation
             B. Assurance that all the objectives dealing with attitudes can be measured
             C. The possibility of incorporating the behavioral sciences into advertising
                 management
             D. A planning tool that can lead to systematic control over advertising
                 budgets and campaigns
             E. None of the above

A   17-42. Which of the following is not a method of pretesting an ad campaign?
             A. Inquiries
             B. Rankings
             C. Projective techniques
             D. Attitude studies
             E. All of the above are pretesting techniques

C   17-43. An advertiser who wants to use a posttest technique would not use the
             _____ technique.
             A. Sales
             B. Recall
             C. Ranking
             D. Recognition
             E. All of the above are posttesting techniques

B   17-44. Attitude studies differ from most pretest techniques in that:
             A. They create an artificial environment and test for success
             B. They deal directly with how people think
             C. They measure the expected sales effectiveness of the advertising effort
             D. Two of the above
             E. All or none of the above

C   17-45. Which of the following is not a pretest-laboratory technique for use in
             evaluating advertising?
             A. Brain-pattern analysis
             B. Galvanic skin response
             C. Recall comprehension
             D. Voice-pitch analysis
             E. Exposure comprehension

E   17-46. Eye tracking as a pretest evaluation technique can:
             A. Aid in determining how to best lay out an ad
             B. Determine the eye movement through an ad
             C. Determine what part of the television scene a person sees first
             D. Determine the focal point of an ad
             E. All of the above

A 17-47. The use of an exposure comprehension advertising pretest would probably be most beneficial to the advertiser using:
A. Mobile media
B. Radio media
C. Television media
D. Newspaper media
E. All of the above

C 17-48. Which of the following is not a classification of a reader as used by STARCH in an ad recognition posttest?
A. Associated reader
B. Nonreader
C. Read-all reader
D. Noted reader
E. None of the above

D 17-49. Advertising registration in a recall posttest is used to measure the number of readers who:
A. Want to see, try, or buy the advertised product
B. Can recall the copy ideas presented by the ad
C. Can indicate the brand or advertiser
D. Can describe the ad without seeing it
E. None of the above

A 17-50. An inquiry posttest would seldom be conducted for ads using the following media vehicle:
A. Outdoor
B. Newspaper
C. Direct mail
D. Cablevision
E. All or none of the above

Completion

17-51. (*Advertising research*) is the systematic gathering, recording, and analyzing of data dealing with the effectiveness of the advertising message and/or its delivery vehicle.

17-52. (*Secondary*) data is information that has already been collected by another source that may be used to solve an advertiser's problem.

17-53. (*Survey*) data collection techniques force the situation by asking questions in order to solicit information. Three major techniques that are used are (*mail*), (*telephone*), and (*personal interview*).

17-54. (*Defining Advertising Goals for Measured Advertising Results*) is an advertising evaluation procedure that compares specific advertising goals with the actual results over time.

17-55. A (*projective*) pretest technique may ask a respondent to assume the identity of a person in an illustration, determine the respondent's makeup through an in-depth interview, or learn what people think through a group interview or focus group.

17-56. The "sweaty palms" test or (_galvanic skin response_) technique works the same way as a "lie-detector" test by means of an electrode attached to the palm and forearm that measures the perspiration level.

17-57. (_Voice-pitch analysis_) is the pretest laboratory technique that measures voice stress as a direct link to emotional reaction.

17-58. The theory behind using (_pupillary analysis_) as a pretest technique is that the pupil of the eye increases if the visual stimulus is of interest to the respondent.

17-59. The (_recall_) posttest technique attempts to measure the impact of an ad on a reader without the person being shown the advertisement.

17-60. The (_inquiry_) posttest technique measures the effectiveness of an ad by means of a split-run test.

CHAPTER 18 - ADVERTISING
AND THE MARKETING PROGRAM

True or False

T   18-1. A firm with a strong marketing plan should have an impact in the marketplace.

T   18-2. A coordinated advertising program results in the desired message appearing in the desired media at the desired time.

F   18-3. A given advertising campaign should only use one advertising theme technique at a time to coordinate the advertising.

T   18-4. Sales promotion must be coordinated with advertising and the sales force as part of the promotion mix.

F   18-5. The PERT planning procedure emphasizes the path which allows the least flexibility in scheduling/coordination.

F   18-6. Horizontal cooperative advertising is an arrangement where a channel of distribution works together to advertise a product.

F   18-7. The goal of horizontal co-op advertising is selective demand.

T   18-8. The idea of cooperative advertising is simple, but its implementation can cause problems.

T   18-9. With cooperative advertising, the product manufacturer and the retail outlet benefit from the joint identity if both parties are strong.

F   18-10. "Double billing" can be a problem in newspaper co-op advertising.

T   18-11. Under the Robinson-Patman Act, the same promotional allowance or co-op program must be offered to all like firms in the marketplace.

F   18-12. Resentment problems in co-op advertising agreements are a result of manufacturer demands.

T   18-13.   Advertising can be used as a selling tool by citing advertising as the reason for purchase.

T   18-14.   Advertising can be promoted as a buyer benefit.

F   18-15.   The inclusion of the <u>Good Housekeeping Seal</u> and the <u>Parents' Seal</u> in advertising for a product has not been very effective for the firms using it.

F   18-16.   Local media rates are a major disadvantage of cooperative advertising.

F   18-17.   Sampling is a form of co-op advertising.

T   18-18.   Coupon misredemption exists when a customer buys a different brand than what the coupon is for and still uses the coupon or when the store submits coupons that were not backed up by a purchase.

F   18-19.   Unlike contests, coupons do work effectively for the advertiser.

T   18-20.   A skill contest should not appear to be impossible to win if the advertiser wants participation.

T   18-21.   One problem with product samples is how much of the product should be given.

T   18-22.   The purpose of trading stamps is to build repeat business.

F   18-23.   In the United States, trading stamps became very popular in the mid-seventies and are still popular today.

F   18-24.   A specialty advertising item is one form of premium.

T   18-25.   Cereal products are heavy users of in-box premiums for children, most of which are heavily promoted on television.

F   18-26.   Firms always use their own products as in-store premiums, such as a free drink with an order of fries and a hamburger.

T   18-27.   Many premiums are used as a continuous promotion to achieve repeat business.

T   18-28.   In some in-store, continuous premium programs, the first item is given free, while additional items are treated as self-liquidators.

T   18-29.   The advantage of a cents-off promotion is that it doesn't appear to inhibit the return to the regular price at a later time.

T   18-30.   Combination offers allow one product to "ride the coattails" of another into the customer's product group.

Multiple Choice

E   18-31.   The marketing plan (a blueprint of the marketing activities planned for a given time period) does not include:
A.   Public relations
B.   Publicity
C.   Personal selling
D.   Sales promotion
E.   All or none of the above

E   18-32.   Coordination within the _____ is vital to the firm.
A.   Marketing mix
B.   Promotion mix
C.   Advertising mix
D.   Two of the above
E.   All of the above

C   18-33.   Which of the following is an example of a format advertising theme?
A.   Wilt Chamberlain for Volkswagen Rabbit
B.   "Coke adds life"
C.   Camel man walking a mile
D.   "Have it your way" at McDonald's
E.   None of the above

A   18-34.   Advertising that stresses the generic product or industry goals and is funded by different firms at the same level of the channel of distribution is known as:
A.   Horizontal cooperative advertising
B.   Coordinated advertising
C.   Vertical cooperative advertising
D.   Logo advertising
E.   None of the above

D   18-35.   A common type of vertical cooperative advertising is:
A.   Manufacturer and retailer
B.   Manufacturer and producer
C.   Wholesaler and retailer
D.   Two of the above
E.   All of the above

B   18-36.   A common user of prorated vertical co-op advertising is the _____ with their typical ad that features numerous products.
A.   Industrial equipment retailer
B.   Supermarket
C.   Tire store
D.   Paint store
E.   All of the above

A   18-37.   A disadvantage associated with vertical co-op advertising is:
A.   Channel resentment
B.   Joint identity
C.   Local rates
D.   Two of the above
E.   All of the above

E   18-38.   All parties get more for their advertising dollar under a co-op arrangement
             because:
             A. The retailer can buy twice as much advertising for a set amount of
                 money
             B. Local ad rates are cheaper than the national rate
             C. The manufacturer can get up to four times as much advertising since
                 many national rates are double the local rate
             D. Two of the above
             E. All of the above

E   18-39.   Channel resentment in a co-op agreement is caused by:
             A. Retailers who are involved in "double billing"
             B. Manufacturers who place too much emphasis on how to get the
                 cheaper local rates
             C. Dealer abuses such as poor placements and waste circulation
             D. Manufacturer stipulations on how the ad should be made up and where
                 it must be run
             E. All of the above

D   18-40.   An advertisement can be merchandised by:
             A. Using an ad to promote the desired personality of the product
             B. Mentioning an ad you placed in an image-making publication when
                 advertising in the traditional media
             C. By including the Good Housekeeping Seal in other advertising once you
                 have placed an ad in that magazine
             D. All of the above
             E. An ad can't be merchandised

C   18-41.   Which of the following is not included in sales promotion?
             A. Price deals
             B. Exhibits
             C. Personal selling
             D. Contests
             E. Sampling

B   18-42.   Which statement concerning coupons is false?
             A. A regular in/on coupon has the best redemption rate of any redemption
                 method.
             B. 95% of the coupon users actively look for coupons.
             C. Over half of all coupons are distributed by means of newspaper.
             D. Coupon usage among households in 1977 was up to 77% from 58% in 1971.
             E. All of the above are true.

A   18-43.   Which of the following is an example of a skill contest sales promotion?
             A. A baking contest
             B. A lottery
             C. A sweepstakes
             D. Two of the above
             E. All of the above

C   18-44. The Federal Trade Commission requires that a contest user reveal all the
        following in the contest rules except:
        A. The conditions, terms, and obligations the winners must adhere to in
            order to receive a prize
        B. The number of prizes to be given
        C. How the list of winners will be distributed to all contestants
        D. The market value of the prizes
        E. The numerical odds of winning each prize

B   18-45. Trading stamps have a better chance of success when:
        A. The target market is urban-oriented
        B. There is a redemption center in the town
        C. The target market is transient
        D. The target market is under 25 years-of-age
        E. All or none of the above

E   18-46. Premiums may be distributed:
        A. In the store
        B. By the manufacturer
        C. With the product
        D. Two of the above
        E. All of the above

C   18-47. In order to generate interest for a product among new customers, a price
        reduction of at least _____ is needed.
        A. 5 percent
        B. 10 percent
        C. 12 percent
        D. 20 percent
        E. 25 percent

E   18-48. Cash rebates have been used to promote:
        A. Hair dryers
        B. Cameras
        C. Turkeys
        D. Two of the above
        E. All of the above

E   18-49. A sales promotion exhibit:
        A. Should encompass both personal selling and advertising in its design
        B. Should be portable
        C. Should be designed to take abuse
        D. Two of the above
        E. All of the above

B   18-50. The purpose of a "tombstone" ad is to:
        A. Sell tombstones
        B. Inform firms about the existence of various promotional allowances
        C. Inform firms about the existence of excess stocks that need to be sold
        D. Inform firms about upcoming legislation that could mean "death" to the
            industry
        E. All or none of the above

18-51.   As a tool of coordination, the (*advertising theme*) can be the uniting force that bridges many diverse ads together in the customer's mind.

18-52.   (*Primary*) demand is the essence of horizontal co-op advertising rather than (*selective*) demand since firms join forces to promote the generic product and industry for the good of all instead of promoting their own brands of the product.

18-53.   The advantages of vertical cooperative advertising are (*local rates*), (*joint identity*), and (*channel encouragement*).

18-54.   A good vertical co-op advertising program should try to minimize the following problem areas: (*lack of control*), (*clerical*), (*legal*), and (*channel resentment*).

18-55.   The nonrecurring or continuous activities which supplement the advertising and personal selling efforts of a firm are called (*sales promotion*).

18-56.   Contests can take two forms: (*skill*) and (*chance*).

18-57.   A premium that requires the customer to pay some amount, such as the premium's actual cost, in addition to providing proof-of-purchase is referred to as a/an (*self-liquidator*).

18-58.   A/An (*price deal*) involves any planned method of price reduction such as cash rebates, cents-off promotions, and combination offers.

18-59.   Eight popular forms of sales promotion are (*coupons*), (*contests*), (*sampling*), (*trading stamps*), (*premiums*), (*price deals*), (*demonstrations*), and (*exhibits*).

18-60.   The (*marketing plan*) is the blueprint of all the marketing activities that are planned for a given period.

CHAPTER 19 - ADVERTISING APPLICATIONS

True or False

T   19-1.   The primary objective of retail advertising is to generate traffic for the store so that personal selling can complete the selling task.

T   19-2.   In terms of advertising, service, location, and image are ways to differentiate a retail store from the competition.

F   19-3.   Direct mail, magazines, and television are the significant advertising vehicles for retailers because of their local orientation.

T   19-4.   Newspaper and radio are quite popular media vehicles for advertising services to consumers.

T   19-5.   The business advertising message tends to be more rational than the consumer advertising message because of the multiple buying influence found in most business situations.

F   19-6.   A good business ad will generate sales volume for the advertiser due to derived demand.

F   19-7.   As is true with retail advertisers, business advertisers normally use an ad agency to help develop their ads.

T   19-8.   Some advertising efforts combine the promotion of a product with that of a service.

T   19-9.   A negative demand for a product implies that people dislike the product enough to be willing to pay to avoid it.

F   19-10.   Full demand is not an unusual situation for most nonprofit organizations.

T   19-11.   The War Advertising Council, which was formed in 1942 to assist in the war effort by disseminating information to the public, has evolved over time into The Advertising Council as we know it today.

F   19-12.   Of all The Ad Council efforts, the Red Cross and Smokey Bear have been the most durable as they date back to World War I.

T   19-13.   Ads for United States Savings Bonds are an example of a national donated campaign.

T   19-14.   A national charity may develop a media approach where all the ads are nationally prepared for implementation on a local basis.

T   19-15.   As with other advertising, political advertising should offer a benefit to the target market.

F   19-16.   The study dealing with advertising impact on state legislature races, as cited in the text, found that less than a third of the respondents indicated that their awareness of a political issue had come through some form of advertising.

F   19-17.   When you advertise the product instead of the firm, you are using institutional advertising.

T   19-18.   An institutional ad directed at the general public would probably be featured on radio or television or in newspapers, while the ad directed at suppliers would more likely be found in the trade magazines.

F   19-19.   Institutional advertising that is aggressive in presenting the position of the firm is known as publicity advertising.

T   19-20.   Credibility is the key to writing good advocacy ads.

T   19-21.   Advocacy advertising can have a negative effect if too much of it is done by a company.

F   19-22.   International advertising refers to the American company that advertises its product in another country while foreign advertising refers to the ads run by the foreign firm in order to sell its products in the United States.

T   19-23.   To avoid the risk of failure, a firm should consider local customs, superstitions, and tastes in its international advertising just as it should recognize these differences when promoting a product in the United States.

T   19-24.   Due to the low literacy rate in some parts of the world, it is important to show on the package what is in the package.

F   19-25.   The media used by international advertisers should not differ from one country to another for a given ad campaign.

T   19-26.   In order to coordinate the advertising effort, a large company selling in many countries should try to use a single advertising agency with a network of offices in the countries the company serves.

F   19-27.   Many marketers believe that the developed countries of the world offer the greatest potential for growth in advertising and marketing in the years to come.

T   19-28.   Multinational firms should promote themselves as firms who promote higher living standards, create new jobs, and provide capital for the country.

T   19-29.   The secret to success in publicity advertising is to get placement in the desired media, but since it is not paid advertising, there is no direct control of placement from the advertiser's standpoint.

F   19-30.   From an international advertising standpoint, the world's largest advertising agency in terms of both gross income and billings is J. Walter Thompson.

Multiple Choice

A   19-31.   Retail advertising is <u>not</u> characterized by:
          A.   Heavy usage of television and magazine advertising
          B.   A relationship between advertising and the store image
          C.   A local orientation
          D.   Two of the above
          E.   None of the above

D   19-32.   The business advertising message should present the buyer benefits that the business customer wants to hear such as:
          A.   Acceptable quality tolerances
          B.   Supplier support
          C.   Continuity of supply
          D.   All of the above
          E.   None of the above

D   19-33.   Business advertisers typically place emphasis on the following media so as to reach the business market without waste circulation:
          A.   Magazines
          B.   Newspapers
          C.   Direct mail
          D.   Two of the above
          E.   All of the above

E 19-34. Services are different from physical products in that:
A. Services are sold before being produced
B. Services may be intangible
C. Services cannot be stored like inventory
D. There is no transfer of ownership in service sales
E. All of the above

E 19-35. A service advertising message would demonstrate dependability, competence, and the ability to meet customer needs by:
A. Using testimonial copy from people in the market area
B. Stating the number of years the firm has been in business
C. Showing the service in action
D. Offering a written guarantee of some type
E. All or none of the above

A 19-36. Which of the following media would tend to be the least effective in advertising services to customers?
A. Outdoor
B. Direct mail
C. Radio
D. Yellow Pages
E. Newspapers

E 19-37. From an organizational standpoint, The Ad Council is:
A. An agency that is funded by the President's Office of Consumer Affairs
B. Coordinated by the National Advertising Review Board (NARB)
C. Housed in the Defense Department as a result of its activities in WW II.
D. A division of the Advertising Checking Bureau
E. None of the above

C 19-38. In order to obtain the assistance of The Ad Council, an organization seeking support for its cause must meet certain qualifications. These do not include:
A. The cause should lend itself to interpretation through advertising methods and media
B. The cause should be nonpartisan, nonsectarian, nonpolitical, and noncommercial
C. The cause should not be anti-business or against the policies of any supporting advertiser or agency
D. The cause should be national in scope but also apply at the local level
E. All or none of the above

A 19-39. The U. S. Postal System and the Volunteer Army are nonprofit organizations that have recently made use of a:
A. National paid campaign
B. Local paid campaign
C. National donated campaign
D. Local donated campaign
E. None of the above

B 19-40. Which of the following media were found to have more impact on the voting
          public in terms of for whom they voted?
          A. Bumper stickers or telephone pole signs
          B. Newspapers or brochures
          C. Television or outdoor posters
          D. Outdoor posters or newspapers
          E. Radio or brochures

E 19-41. A form of public relations advertising is:
          A. Advocacy advertising
          B. Institutional advertising
          C. Publicity advertising
          D. Two of the above
          E. All or none of the above

C 19-42. Which of the following is not a typical objective or goal of public relations
          advertising?
          A. Arouse the interest of stockholders and the financial community
          B. Inform and serve customers
          C. Create a favorable image for a product
          D. Render a public service
          E. Win the goodwill of community neighbors and dealers

E 19-43. An example of public relations advertising is:
          A. A firm is advertised instead of a product
          B. The promotion of an idea that is favorable to a company
          C. The development of news stories for use by the press
          D. Two of the above
          E. All of the above

E 19-44. A popular theme for an institutional advertisement stresses the:
          A. Services provided and benefits offered to customers, suppliers, etc.
          B. Economic impact of the firm on the community
          C. Sizable investment made in plant facilities and equipment
          D. Company sponsorship of a softball team
          E. All or none of the above

E 19-45. Depending on the campaign objective, an effective media vehicle to use
          for advocacy advertising is:
          A. Print media
          B. Television
          C. Direct mail
          D. Only two of the above
          E. All of the above

A 19-46. The publicity advertising press kit fact sheet would most likely not include:
          A. Information on product prices
          B. Information dealing with buyer benefits
          C. Date of product introduction or other significant dates
          D. Information pertinent to the local area
          E. Information on the company

B   19-47.   Considering both cultural and legal factors, a multinational firm should work to promote its image as an organization that strives to:
        A. Bring managerial talent to the country
        B. Promote higher living standards
        C. Export capital from the country
        D. Two of the above
        E. All or none of the above

D   19-48.   In terms of international advertising, local pride (nationalism) should be considered where developing:
        A. Ads
        B. Products
        C. Packages
        D. Two of the above
        E. All or none of the above

C   19-49.   In terms of international advertising, which of the following statements is false?
        A. Countries do not have uniform trademark and copyright requirements.
        B. Comparative advertising is not permitted in some countries.
        C. Due to language differences and literacy problems, pictures have been found to be the only safe way to communicate an idea in an ad.
        D. Colors mean different things in different cultures.
        E. Whenever possible, it is wise to show nationals of a country in ads that are developed for that country.

C   19-50.   In terms of international advertising, which of the following statements is false?
        A. A trade fair is a good way to promote a product in a soviet-bloc country.
        B. Movie theaters in Europe are a strong media choice.
        C. Commercial television is the best way to reach the population in Sweden.
        D. Dentsu, Inc. is the world's largest ad agency.
        E. Advertising is taxed in different ways, thereby causing advertising to be very expensive in some countries.

Completion

19-51.   (*Retail*) advertising is advertising by a firm that sells to the ultimate consumer.

19-52.   (*Service*) advertising is advertising that sells an intangible that requires no transfer of ownership to complete the sale.

19-53.   (*Publicity*) advertising is a form of public relations advertising whose purpose is to present the story of the organization in news form.

19-54.   Advertising that attempts to sell an idea that is favorable to the organization is known as (*advocacy*) advertising, which is part of a larger category of advertising known as (*public relations*) advertising.

19-55.   (*Public relations*) is defined as the business of inducing the public to have understanding for and goodwill toward a person, firm, or institution.

19-56. A collection of facts and figures, photographs, and other information about an organization which is used for publicity advertising purposes is known as a/an (*press kit*).

19-57. The (*Advertising Council*) is a voluntary organization that coodinates the development of nonprofit advertising campaigns on the national level.

19-58. In terms of advertising expenditures per capita, the country with the largest per capita spending level is the (*United States*). The country with the next highest level of spending is (*Bermuda*). (The data for these statements is based on the information given in the text - 1976 data as published in 1979.)

19-59. According to 1978 gross income and billings data, the largest advertising agency in the world is (*Dentsu, Inc.*).

19-60. When a German firm advertises its product line in the United States, it is involved in an advertising application known as (*International*) advertising.

CHAPTER 20 - ADVERTISING TRENDS

True or False

F 20-1. A study of advertising trends reveals that few changes will be seen in advertising in the years to come.

T 20-2. The only certain element in the future of advertising is change.

F 20-3. Studies indicate that the marketplace population in the year 2000 will be comprised mainly of highly-educated young singles.

F 20-4. Though buyer benefits do not sell products today, studies indicate that they will sell products by the year 2000.

T 20-5. The lawyer will become an important part of any advertising team as advertising regulation increases.

F 20-6. The advertising regulatory bodies are expected to continue to increase the level of creative freedom for the advertiser of the future.

F 20-7. Before the year 2000, $180 billion will be spent on advertising on an annual basis in the U. S. due to inflation and growth.

T 20-8. By the year 2000, a fee system is expected to be in wide use in the advertising industry.

T 20-9. Due to cost considerations, many existing small advertising agencies will be acquired by larger firms in the years to come or will go out of business.

F 20-10. Advertisers hope that the future will provide a new Robinson Act that will provide trademark protection while a product is being developed.

T   20-11.   In terms of the future, additional efforts will be made to write copy by formula.

F   20-12.   In the future, more advertisers will use outside special service firms due to the high cost of in-house ad production.

T   20-13.   In the future, computer systems will be used more in the production of ads, as well as to transmit the ad to the media and the audience.

F   20-14.   Most advertisers believe that magazines will be the major advertising media in the year 2000.

T   20-15.   Television and various forms of direct media will be significant media forms for the advertiser in the year 2000.

T   20-16.   If an increase in the price of gasoline keeps more families out of their cars, then transit media should become more significant as a media choice for more advertisers.

F   20-17.   In terms of the future, outdoor media will have less exposure if there are more cars on the road.

F   20-18.   Talking displays are the next logical step in the future of point-of-purchase advertising.

T   20-19.   In terms of the future of advertising, it is believed that the cost-per-thousand (CPM) exposures calculation will continue to be important to the advertiser as media costs escalate.

T   20-20.   In terms of the future, one of the most significant media trends will be a more careful scrutiny of all media by an advertiser.

F   20-21.   The future shows a definite trend towards finally measuring the sales effectiveness of advertising.

T   20-22.   The use of co-op advertising is expected to be quite significant in the years ahead.

F   20-23.   The growth of computer use in business should eliminate the traditional percentage-of-sales budgeting procedure.

F   20-24.   Though both posttest and pretest research methodologies will be important in the future, more emphasis will be placed on posttesting.

T   20-25.   The advertising of services is a growth area for the future since the service sector is growing at a faster rate than marketing in general.

T   20-26.   In some instances the advertising manager will be more a sales manager than an advertiser.

T   20-27.   The public relations director should create publicity for the advertiser through news stories and press releases.

F   20-28. One of the most important jobs in an advertising organization is copywriting
             since it aids in the development of the advertising foundation as well as
             ad development and media selection.

T   20-29. Career preparation in advertising may include a college degree, work
             experience in selling, and the development of a sample portfolio.

F   20-30. In the advertising industry, the media representative is often referred to
             as the media buyer.

Multiple Choice

E   20-31. The areas of advertising that will undergo change in the future include:
             A. Media
             B. Industry
             C. Management
             D. None of the above
             E. All of the above

C   20-32. All of the following were marketplace characteristics of the ten year period
             prior to 1976 as cited by E. B. Weiss in Advertising Age except:
             A. The consumer movement became significant
             B. Lowest birth rate in U. S. history
             C. The marriage rate went up
             D. The hippie subculture revolutionized society
             E. Women's lib became a reality.

A   20-33. McCann-Erickson has predicted that the $100 billion advertising plateau
             of annual expenditures by all firms will be reached before the year:
             A. 1985
             B. 1990
             C. 1995
             D. 2000
             E. None of the above

A   20-34. The following statement concerning the future of the advertising industry
             is false.
             A. The small ad agency will disappear by the year 2000.
             B. Large full-service ad agencies will be more prevalent.
             C. The industry will see a de-emphasis on advertising commissions.
             D. Creative freedom will be reduced by an increase in advertising
                 regulations.
             E. All or none of the above

D   20-35. A de-emphasis on advertising commissions may result in:
             A. A widely-used fee system in the industry
             B. More noncommissioned media being used
             C. More large full-service agencies being prevalent
             D. Two of the above
             E. All or none of the above

D   20-36. In terms of the future, advertisers will continue to search for the one
             best way to develop a/an:
             A. Identifying symbol
             B. Advertisement
             C. Package
             D. All of the above
             E. None of the above

B   20-37. Advertisers hope to provide trademark protection for a product while it
             is being developed by means of a new:
             A. Robinson Act
             B. Lanham Act
             C. Lanagan Act
             D. Robinson-Patman Act
             E. None of the above

D   20-38. In terms of the future, more agencies will begin to produce in-house ads
             due to the:
             A. Cost of outside production
             B. Decrease in the number of special service firms
             C. Flexibility provided by an in-house arrangement
             D. Two of the above
             E. All of the above

E   20-39. In terms of the future, computer systems will be used increasingly by
             advertisers except for:
             A. Transmitting the finished ad to the media
             B. Processing the photographs for the ads
             C. Setting type and developing layouts for an ad
             D. Sending the final ad to the audience
             E. All or none of the above

A   20-40. An advertiser can expect the major media in the year 2000 to include all
             the following except:
             A. Magazines
             B. Cable television
             C. Television
             D. Forms of direct mail
             E. All or none of the above

C   20-41. The following statement concerning the future of magazines as a major
             media form is false.
             A. Magazines may resort to smaller circulations to reduce expenses.
             B. Magazines are getting smaller or are being made part of the electronic
                 media.
             C. Due to a cost increase, magazines will get larger.
             D. A magazine advertiser can expect less reach per ad.
             E. All or none of the above

D   20-42. The future of the mobile media indicates that:
             A. More autos will be used for advertising
             B. Outdoor advertising will be concentrated in the central city
             C. Transit media should grow in use
             D. Two of the above
             E. All of the above

C   20-43.   The key word in an advertiser's future seems to be:
          A.   Management
          B.   Skill
          C.   Change
          D.   Variety
          E.   None of the above

A   20-44.   In terms of the future, a more careful scrutiny of all media by an
          advertiser will be made due to:
          A.   Escalating media costs
          B.   Cost per thousand exposures
          C.   A budgetary requirement
          D.   Two of the above
          E.   All of the above

D   20-45.   In terms of the future, advertising research will continue to be important
          due to the:
          A.   Advertiser's need for assurance that his ads are effective
          B.   Complete lack of advertising effectiveness
          C.   Amount of money spent on advertising
          D.   Two of the above
          E.   All of the above

A   20-46.   The advertising manager of a firm would typically not:
          A.   Develop the text for an ad
          B.   Serve as a liaison officer with an ad agency
          C.   Head up the sales staff of a radio station or magazine
          D.   See that the actual campaign is created if an agency isn't used
          E.   None of the above

D   20-47.   In planning for a career in advertising, it is helpful if a person has:
          A.   A college degree
          B.   A sample portfolio
          C.   Outside work experience such as selling
          D.   Two of the above is better than one
          E.   All of the above are essential

B   20-48.   An art director should have primary responsibility for all the following
          except:
          A.   Photographs and drawings
          B.   The production of the ad
          C.   The application of design principles
          D.   Two of the above
          E.   All or none of the above

C   20-49.   The media buyer should take into account all of the following except:
          A.   The overall impact of each media
          B.   Reach and frequency of the ad
          C.   The visual aspects of the ad
          D.   Discounts offered by the media
          E.   Availability of the media

D   20-50.   A media salesperson or media rep:
       A.   May create the ads to be used in the media
       B.   Calls on advertisers and agencies to sell space or time
       C.   Should use the discounts offered by the media
       D.   Two of the above
       E.   All of the above

Completion

20-51.   McCann-Erickson predicts that by the year (_1985_), the $100 billion advertising expenditure level will be reached as a result of both growth and inflation.

20-52.   A type of (_fee system_) should become quite popular in the future as the advertising industry moves away from the commission system of compensation.

20-53.   In terms of the future of advertising research, more emphasis will be placed on (_pretesting_) as advertisers attempt to be certain that their ads are as effective as possible before any significant sum of money is spent on advertising.

20-54.   The only thing certain about advertising is (_change_).

20-55.   The (_account executive_) is the agency employee who coordinates all agency activities with the advertiser.

20-56.   The (_advertising manager_) is the head of the advertising department who serves as liaison officer with the agency. Also may be the person who heads up the sales department for the media firm.

20-57.   The (_media buyer_) is the person who is charged with the responsibility to implement the media plan.

20-58.   Career preparation for advertising includes a/an (_college degree_), (_work experience_), and (_sample portfolio_).

20-59.   If a person wants to work for an advertising agency, a good source for names to send a letter and resume to is the directory entitled: (_Standard Directory of Advertising Agencies_).

20-60.   If you are looking for a career at the core of business, if you enjoy working with imaginative people, if you can solve problems under pressure, if the challenge of winning the public's attention through effective communication excites you, and if you are not afraid to assume responsibility and make decisions, then you should consider (_advertising_) as a career.